YOUR RELATIONSHIPS & NETWORKS

Connected For Destiny

Book # 3 From The "Seasoned For Destiny" Series

Sally Mahihu

Your Relationships and Networks

ISBN: 978-9914-9886-3-5

Copyright © 2020 © 2022 by Sally Mahihu

P. O. Box 4317-00200 Nairobi

Mobile No: 0722 820 969

Published in Kenya by

House of Wealth Publishers

+254 737 405 827

houseofwealthpublishers@gmail.com

Table of Contents

Chapter One

Connected For Destiny..

Wisdom Nuggets for Relating Effectively

Chapter Two

The Paradoxical Destiny Woman.............................

Owning Your Absurdity Without Apology

Chapter Three

The Destiny Helpers of a Vision Bearer....................

Nurturing the Relationships that Propel You to Destiny

Chapter Four

The Destiny Killers of a Destiny Carrier..................

Neutralizing the Forces that Fight Your Destiny

Chapter Five

The Sibling Rivals In a Destiny Family.....................

Diffusing Family Conflicts that Threaten Your Destiny

Chapter Six

Mastering The Art Of Negotiation..........................

Seeking Mutually Beneficial Outcomes in Your Relationships

Dedication

I dedicate this book to every woman of destiny who often struggles in relating to herself and others. I am confident that in time you will learn to connect to yourself and to others for the sake of your destiny.

Acknowledgement

First and foremost, I would like to thank God for enabling me to write and finish this Book Series. I pray these books will impact and bless many Women who are determined to fulfil their Destiny.

I would like to thank my **Husband Ngari** who really "gets me" and who I refer to as my "Destiny Spouse" because indeed he is a true gift from God and he has been supportive beyond measure during the course of my writing, these Books, in more ways than I can count.

My **sons Eric and Chris**, who are truly sons of my strength, and who have also supported and encouraged me in my "Destiny endeavours" no matter how radically insane I sounded at times.

My late **Dad, Chris Kahara** who constantly affirmed me and instilled the confidence I needed to embark on many "Destiny journeys" leading to where and who I am today.

Rev Teresa Wairimu, my "Destiny Midwife" who has spoken into my life for the past two decades and who has been diligent in nurturing, moulding and shaping me, to birth out the gifts within me (even during the times when my own foolishness and short-sightedness, coupled with a zeal that was often devoid of knowledge threatened to abort my Purpose and Calling.)

H.E. Madam Rachel Ruto who is equally passionate about the empowerment of women and who I admire and respect tremendously for her continuous and tireless commitment to better the lives of women in our society and Nation.

My Aunt Rev Judy Mbugua for believing in me and for being a pillar of strength to me for over the years as a mother figure, for teaching me that my roles as a wife and mother are not an excuse for, but rather an incentive to fulfil my Purpose and Destiny.

My friend and Mentor Dr. Herta Von Stigel who came into my life, at just the right time and helped me to understand that I needed to conquer the Mountain within me before I could conquer the Mountains around me, and whose invaluable friendship and mentorship is a great source of encouragement for me.

My diligent research Assistants and Typists **Victor M. Mwangi, Frida Wanjira** and **Tecla Karimi** who all worked tirelessly in making these books happen.

My Publisher & Cover Designer Shadrack Radido of House Of Wealth Publishers who allowed me the freedom I needed in this Series of Books even when I stubbornly chose to deviate from the traditional Book writing ethics and who has been a solid sounding board on the many technical issues regarding this Series.

My Editor Dr. Mark Stibbe for his excellent editing and no-nonsense professional approach, truly a gift in the literary world.

My die-hard Spice Girls and faithful Women from my Seasoned Woman Vision who cheer me on and whose undeterred insistent claims that there is still more in me for them than I let out, warms my heart and provokes me to keep doing that which I was created for.

Everyone else who contributed in one way or another to the conception and birthing of this Series of Books.

Foreword

I have known Sally for over two decades now from the time she joined and begun to serve me in Ministry. Sally is a very zealous and passionate Woman in whatever she believes in.

Beyond her professional career as a Lawyer, Sally has demonstrated strong gifts of speaking, teaching, mentoring and writing and over the years I have often encouraged her to unleash these gifts. I am extremely proud to see that she has finally done so in these Books **"SEASONED FOR DESTINY"** and I am confident that she will go on to author many more for the benefit of this generation and the generations to come.

Sally has a distinct Call to the Women in the Marketplace for whom has an undeniable burden, and her ability to reach out and offer herself to those women who suffer in silence, totally closed up, yet they really need someone they can trust and open up to.

Sally has addressed every type of Woman in these Books and the topics and subjects she has chosen to address are of great interest so she will reach and impact a very wide margin of Women, across the divide, locally and globally.

In other words, Sally has covered literally every subject that every Woman needs, to become well equipped and empowered for fulfilling Purpose and Destiny. More importantly she has done it in a manner that every Woman will identify with, because she has delved into the core basics of every issue without sugar coating the seriousness that one will require to commit to this journey to Destiny. Yet at the same time she has strongly encouraged every Woman by laying out the roadmap and by affirming and assuring her again and again, that she already has what it takes to master this journey and fulfil her Destiny.

Women from every sphere and sector will be awakened to the significance of their Callings and Destiny, giving them the incentive and motivation, they needed to forge on without giving up.

I have been in Christian ministry for over 45 years now and I have been humbled and privileged to minister to thousands of people Worldwide and to lead an organization with over 10, 000 partners locally and globally. The messages in these Books are central to the gospel that I myself preach because Destiny is God ordained.

I have no doubt that everyone who will read these Books will be greatly impacted and transformed, empowered and equipped to arise and lay hold of and fulfil that Destiny that each was born for.

Rev. Teresia Wairimu Kinyanjui.

Director& Founder,

Faith Evangelistic Ministry (FEM).

Endorsement

Destiny is one of the most misunderstood concepts today. Needless to say, the very mention of this word elicits feelings of inadequacy and anxiety among many. This has mainly been because of the complexity and mystery that seems to surround the understanding of what destiny is or is not.

In the 'Seasoned for Destiny' series, Sally wholeheartedly deliberates on the tenets that are to bring flavor and color to one's life. Reading through the pages it is clear that she empties her heart seeking to touch a heart at a time. This series specifically address the internal struggles that become stumbling blocks in the way of success for many and in particular women.

In today's world where everything is fast-paced and we all are confronted with many options; it is prudent that one finds their space and balance in life. Reading this book will motivate you to take a personal stock of where you are in the journey to destiny while recognizing and fixing the hindrances on the way.

To live a life of meaning and significance understanding Destiny is not an option but an expectation. As one who is passionate about women empowerment, I concur that clarity of purpose and calling, the fortitude to make available connections and the resilience to maintain success on the path of destiny can be overwhelming. This series is therefore an essential tool for one to make this valuable journey.

Her Excellency,

Rachel Ruto.

Spouse of the Deputy President,

Republic of Kenya.

Endorsement

I have known Sally from when she was about 5 years old and our relationship is firstly that of a mother and daughter. Beyond our family ties and now that Sally has grown to be a wife and mother with her own home, we have become very close friends and prayer partners and we are a great support and strength to one another in this journey to Destiny.

From an early age, Sally has demonstrated such a strong gift of expression and articulation. Sally is undeniably a gifted and anointed Servant of God who ministers the gospel passionately. She is also an inspirational coach and mentor to many women and girls from every walk of life. Her marketplace ministry has impacted many far and wide.

When Sally birthed her Seasoned Woman Forum about 7 years ago and as I witnessed her teachings, mentorship and coaching programs, I knew it would just be a matter of time before she consolidated those valuable teachings into books to reach a wider audience and sphere.

I think that every woman reading this book who will be transformed radically and propelled to fulfilling her Purpose and Destiny.

I am very passionate for Families and Nations, and a firm believer that strong healthy families are the foundation of strong healthy Nations. So, as I read these Books, I was deeply affected and encouraged by the manner in which Sally has tied up the value of the woman, not only as a leader, wealth creator, professional, career woman, but also as a family-oriented woman.

Any woman serious about fulfilling her Purpose and Destiny must be able to align her role as a family woman with her Purpose and Destiny and she must be cognizant of the fact that she cannot effectively impact Nations without first impacting families.

This series of books addresses every woman of every race, creed and color, and from any society and Nation, who desires to be and do all that she was born and created for.

Sally has adequately highlighted literally every dilemma and problem that a woman will encounter in the course of fulfilling her Purpose and Destiny, irrespective of her social status and standing in life, and she has given very practical solutions to these dilemmas and problems.

I would therefore urge every woman to read this Series of Books not only for her own equipping and empowerment but also for the equipping and empowerment of other women who she will share the contents of these book with.

Rev. Dr Judy Mbugua.

The Founder of the Homecare Spiritual Fellowship.

Endorsement

Sally Mahihu's book series "Seasoned for Destiny" is a clarion call for every woman, regardless of age, race or tribe, to discover her true identity, live out her deeper purpose and leave a legacy that younger generations are proud to remember. This book series is for such as time as this!"

Dr Herta von Stiegel, author of *The Mountain Within – Leadership Lessons and Inspiration for your Climb to the Top.*

Endorsement

I am glad that Sally has followed through in writing this series of books titled **"Seasoned for Destiny"**. A couple of years ago, I gave her a word which I had received from the lord, that she would write some very significant books on issues pertaining to women in the marketplace.

These books will encourage and guide women greatly in understanding certain fundamentals that are related to their destiny such as business, career, leadership, relationships etc. Sally has captured literally every aspect of a modern woman's life, and she has taken time to address and analyze these issues in a way that every woman can identify with.

Sally has left no stone unturned in candidly addressing the subtle and not so subtle issues that often derail and delay many women from unleashing their full potential, to enable them to bring out their best selves.

I am persuaded that these books will change the lives of many women and will equip a new generation to become powerful agents of transformation in their spheres of influence.

Rev. Steve Pailthorpe

President of Crown Global, CEO of Iconic Digital & Senior Pastor of Crown Family Church

Introduction

I am fully persuaded that once a Woman understands who she was born to be and embraces the reason she was created (the Purpose for her being), then she will begin to live purposefully and intentionally towards it, and attain true fulfilment. And in so doing she will not only lay hold of her own Destiny, but she will also impact and propel many people, societies and Nations to their Purpose and Destiny as well.

This Series known as **"Seasoned For Destiny"** consists of 5 Books namely *Book 1 Your Naming and Defining, Book 2 Your Calling and Positioning, Book 3 Your Relationships and Networks, Book 4 Your Making and Shaping* and *Book 5 Your Harvests and Legacy.*

BOOK 1 titled *"Your Naming and Defining"* deals with a Woman's identity, understanding **"the who"** she was born to be, it addresses her ability to embrace her true and authentic self. The chapters in this Book expound the various fundamentals regarding Identity and the power of Naming; The Passwords to your true identity (understanding what should and what should not define you). The Triggers to an Identity Crisis, The Diary of a Destiny Diva, The Voices that shape and define you, The Destiny Queen or the Destiny Quitter, The Destiny Preserver or the Destiny Destroyer, The Destiny Clinger or the Destiny Kisser, The Destiny Connector or the Destiny Blocker, The Global Destiny Carrier or the Local Destiny Carrier, The Destiny Respecter or the Destiny Despiser,

The Eagle Destiny or the Chicken Destiny, The Diary of a Destiny Diva and The Daily Confessions of a Destiny Chaser (on how to reinforce and affirm your identity daily with positive decrees and declarations).

BOOK 2 titled *"Your Calling and Positioning"* deals with a Woman's Calling and Purpose namely how to discover **"the what"** she was created to do, how to birth it and safeguard it, having a deep insight of what her purpose and calling entails, understanding how to access what she needs to fulfil it. This Book also it looks at the Woman's Positioning and Alignment on how to locate **"the where"** (in terms of sector or sphere) she is ordained to impact, how to navigate in that specific area and how to establish herself there. The chapters in this particular Book address the pertinent factors about Calling and Positioning namely; The Cues and Clues to her Calling, The Realities About her Calling, The Tools of a true Visionary, The steps to Birthing her Visions to Destiny, The Steps after Birthing her Visions to Destiny, The Pebble Stones in your High Heels to Destiny, The Arrows to her Place and sphere, The Snags and Snares in her Place and sphere, Establishing herself in the Place of Assignment and The Key Roles Of A Destiny Woman.

BOOK 3 titled *"Your Relationships And Networks"* deals with a Woman's relationships (networks and associations) namely **"the whom"** she should connect to, or disconnect from, for the sake of her Destiny. The chapters in this Book address; The Paradoxes In A Destiny Woman, Your Destiny Helpers, Your Destiny Killers, Your Sibling Rivals, Mastering The Art of Negotiation, The Spice Girls and Your Suspect Suitors.

BOOK 4 titled *"Your Making and Shaping"* deals with a Woman's moulding and sculpturing for Destiny namely **"the How"** of her preparation and equipping, and the various tests and trials she needs to undergo in order to fulfil her Purpose and Call as well as the principles, values and habits that inform her choices and decisions and refine her for Destiny. The chapters in this Book address and include; The Storms of a Destiny Survivor, The Scars of a Sculptured Woman, The Pain Patterns of a Destiny Champion, The Shape of a Destiny Diamond, The Trademarks of a Destiny Vessel, The Habits of a Destiny Addict, The Elegance of an Eagle Woman and The Pit-stops of a Destiny Racer.

BOOK 5 titled *"Your Harvests and Legacy"* deals with a Woman's legacy and the footprints she leaves behind for her generation and future generations. The chapters in this Book include; The Seasons Of a Destiny Sower, Your Harvest In 7 Areas, Facts About Your Harvest, Hindrances To Your Harvest, Threats To Your Harvest, How To Respond To Your Harvest, Reasons Why You Get The Harvest, The Purpose Of Your Harvest, The Marks Of A Destiny Legend and A Woman's Defining Decades.

One of the main reasons for writing this Book was to consolidate the Principles that I have been teaching, coaching and mentoring on over the years with regard to Purpose and Destiny.

Perhaps another compelling reason for writing this Series of Books is that every issue addressed here resonates within me personally, because these are issues I or people very close to me, continue to grapple with, and my sharing them here is for purposes of identifying my own personal struggles with those of the women I am addressing.

It is my sincere desire and hope that those who read this Series of Books will use the teachings to propel themselves to Destiny and to pass them on to other women, including those they are training, mentoring and coaching. These Books will also form very valuable material for discussion groups whether as Book clubs, diverse groups within churches, corporate organisations and in all the various sectors and spheres of influence and hence the reason I have inserted "Destiny questions to ponder on" at the end of each chapter so that the interactive discussions can have a real impact on each reader and hopefully provoke them to apply the guidelines offered here in fulfilling their Purpose and Calling.

My sincere hope and expectation is that these Books are going to equip and empower every Woman desirous of fulfilling Purpose and to edify and assure her that no matter how hard the journey has been and no matter how much she has wanted to give up, she indeed has what it takes to finish this journey because she was designed for Destiny and she is already seasoned for it.

Although the target audience of this Series is primarily Women, it is now clear to me that even the men who come across them it will be equally impacted and equipped by the universal principles and the various topics addressed.

It is also my intention to target the young woman (older teens and young adults) because most of these principles and issues will greatly help these young women to avoid the mistakes that many of us older women made in our early years, and it will hopefully help the young woman to also avoid unnecessary delays in her journey to Destiny. It is therefore my sincere hope and prayer that every woman, young and old will read this Series of Books and be propelled to her Destiny.

The most fundamental aspect when embarking on your journey to Destiny is knowing "the **who you were born to be**" and coming to a place where you embrace your true and authentic self and walk securely in it because everything else thereafter regarding your Destiny hinges on this first revelation about your true self-identity.

These Books address, every Woman at whatever place she may be in her quest for Purpose and Destiny, the late Destiny bloomer, the Destiny dreamer and Destiny chaser, the Destiny wagon, the Destiny spectator, the Destiny backslider.

These Women are all desirous of living purposefully but they each struggle with different aspects about Destiny, whereby some may struggle with knowing and discovering 'the who' and 'the what' they were created to be (their self-identity and Calling), they go round in circles seeking 'the where' they were assigned to influence (their place and sphere of assignment) and 'the whom' they were designed to relate and connect with (the relationships), many of them get blindsided by the how they get made and formed (tests, trials and tribulations), while others navigate life steering dangerously without a road map seeking 'the which' (values and principles) they need to get there, while others become lethargic and burnout because they lack a sufficient conviction that the journey is worth the high price and sacrifice, they seem to be paying.

Every Woman's future after reading this Series of Books will be brightened by her assurance and confidence that she can now become the who she was born to be, do the what she was created to do, locate and position herself where she was sent to be an influence, relate and connect with the people that were assigned for her, surrender and embrace the process that will mould and make her into a vessel fit for Destiny, walk and align with the principles and values that she was intended to use to usher her to Destiny, lay hold of and effectively manage the successes, rewards and harvests that come with her faithfulness and diligence and leave footprints that will be a positive legacy for her generation and future generations.

What Is To Be Seasoned For Destiny?

For Purposes of this series of Books being "**Seasoned**" does not mean you have accomplished and "**arrived**" rather it means that you are passionate enough to lay hold of your Destiny, that you are ready to step forth by faith and embark on this epic journey just as you are; with the assurance that as you do so, the equipping and empowering you seek or need will be part and parcel of the journey.

... **"Being Seasoned for Destiny"** means that even though you occasionally struggle with who you are in the midst of a tumultuous dispensation that often seeks to swallow and drown you... **YET** you tenaciously fight to keep your head up, knowing that there is only one of you, and the only one you need to be, the one you were born to be.

... **"Being Seasoned for Destiny"** means that even though there are many raw and rough edges in your Character, that are still undergoing moulding and shaping... **YET** you continue to submit yourself to the skilful hands of the Master Potter, knowing that a **"Choice Vessel"** like you, will take longer to be formed because of the great impact and influence you will have on Nations and Generations.

... **"Being Seasoned for Destiny"** means that even though you have not quite mastered the Storms of life like failed relationships, chronic failures, loneliness, self-doubt and rejection, just to mention a few... **YET** you continue to brace yourself against those storms, choosing to dance in the rain; knowing that as you continue to set your sail in the wind of hope then ultimately, those storms will in fact become the very forces that will strengthen and propel you and bring you to that higher place of being alone, but not lonely, a place of self-knowledge, self-acceptance and self-assurance.

.... **"Being Seasoned for Destiny"** means that even though the seed of your womb has not germinated into the **"Daughters of Substance"** and **"Sons of Strength"** you had hoped for... **YET** you remain expectant that irrespective of any shortcomings in your parenting skills, or any unjust twist of fate, your resilience as a praying mother is never in vain and in due season, your Sons and Daughters will manifest into a Seasoned Generation, that will shake cities and impact Nations.

… **"Being seasoned for Destiny"** means that even though you may constantly be in a financial mess and distress, until you feel so desperate and drained… **YET** you refuse to despair knowing that your hands are anointed to create wealth and as you continue to trust, embrace and practice sound godly wealth creating habits and principles, then surely the floodgates of heaven will fling open and usher you into unprecedented financial freedom.

… **"Being Seasoned for Destiny "**means that even though the dire consequences of your **poor choices**, have come to haunt you and you are paying the painful price of your past folly under a heavy cloak of remorse… **YET** you keep your head lifted up high knowing that as you appreciate the lessons learned from your past folly, then this too will pass; because your harsh and ugly Winter must ultimately surrender to your soft and beautiful Spring that will come with forbearance and Second Chances.

… **"Being Seasoned for Destiny"** means that perhaps your inner joy is being dampened by the anguish and agony of a sick body…. **YET** you forge on, smiling through your pain knowing that as long as you have a Purpose and Assignment, that you are committed to fulfil and a Destiny to lay hold of, then your Creator will preserve you and keep you, until you are done.

…**"Being Seasoned for Destiny"** means that even though your walk with God is like a seesaw, characterised by some seasons of intense (almost fanatical) passion and commitment and a radical faith, but also with other seasons of panic, doubt, or even silent indignation when things do not go the way you thought… **YET** you pick yourself up every time and dust off the doubt and purge your panic, and with hot blinding tears, you make a decision to hope and trust anyway, knowing that He who began a good work in you is able to complete it.

…"**Being Seasoned For Destiny**" means that even though you have encountered Chronic failures and disappointment… YET it is about finding the grace to deal with the many disappointments of life and finding the resolve to regain missed seasons and lost opportunities, it is about finding the strength to reposition yourself for a new beginning, because a Seasoned Woman knows, that while there is life, there is hope and while there is hope, there is always another chance to rise again and forge on to fulfil her Destiny.

… "**Being Seasoned for Destiny**" means that even though you come to the end of yourself YET your find a song in your heart that keeps you going when the journey gets tough and this is the song that will keep her going even when the storms rage and the fiery furnace flares.

The Seasoned Woman knows…

Who she really is…?

The Purpose for which she was created…

She is uniquely gifted…

She does not allow her failures…

And successes to define her…

She confidently says…

When I grow up I want to be Me!

The Seasoned Woman knows…

She is fearfully and wonderfully made…

With a true beauty inside her…

Reflected in her whole life lived…

The Seasoned Woman clothes herself…

In dignity, honesty, integrity, patience, kindness, mercy and love…

The Seasoned Woman has learnt…

To embrace the seasons of her life…

Allow them to mould and sculpt her…

Into a vessel of strength, honour and dignity…

She is a Woman of all Seasons…

A vessel of strength, honour and dignity...

She has learnt to weather and survive the storms of her daily life...

Having the grace to dance in the rain...

To smile through her pain...

She has risen to define life...

The strength to rise like a phoenix from the ashes...

The Seasoned Woman has passion for her Nation...

She has solutions for her Generation...

And she has the welfare of her people at heart...

She is a voice to the voiceless...

Therefore, as you reflect and take stock of all the myriad of seasons you may have encountered so far in your journey to destiny, remember that you are "**So Totally Seasoned**" for your Destiny and that nothing shall by any means prevent you, from finishing your race and not only finishing it, but finishing strong... So, soldier on **Woman of Destiny**, until you reach the finish line.

Chapter One

CONNECTED FOR DESTINY

Wisdom Nuggets for Relating Effectively

Chapter Preview

1) *Knowing When To Adopt Strategic Silence And Tactical Retreats*

2) *Knowing How To Deal With Those You No Longer Trust*

3) *Knowing Your Value And Relevance Despite Your Weaknesses*

4) *Knowing How To Become Collateral Damage For A Greater Goal*

5) *Knowing when to have "no opinion" in a matter*

6) *Knowing how to extract the good in others and discard the rest*

7) *Knowing how to conceal your greatness with "divine foolishness"*

OPENING REMARKS

Your connecting, relates to the very crucial relationships, networks and associations that you will need to develop and maintain in order to fulfil your Calling and Destiny.

"We don't meet people by accident, they are meant to cross our path for a reason." ~ **Kathryn Perez**

As a Woman of Destiny and as you seek to fulfil your Purpose, one of the most fundamental tools and resources you will require are relationships and divine connections.

- There will be those people who are your Destiny Seed namely protégés, assignees, mentees, coaches, etc. that you have been called to impact, transform and usher to their Destiny.
- There will be those people namely your Destiny helpers, like burden bearers, ladders holders, sponsors, connectors, intercessors, gate keepers, etc. who have been assigned to help and usher you to your own Destiny.
- There will also be those people namely time and Destiny wasters, who have nothing to do with your Destiny and they are not your portion.
- There will also be those people namely Destiny killers, like saboteurs, assassins, destroyers, derailers, blockers etc. bent on killing your Destiny at every turn in your journey.

Among those relationships, there will be your professional colleagues, your business associates, your co-investors, your social networks, your family members and relatives, your intimate romantic relationships, your ministerial church co-workers, your work place colleagues etc. And all these will impact your Destiny in one way or another and it will be your sole responsibility to discern and identify them and relate to them appropriately for the sake of your Calling and Destiny.

"The most important things are the connections you make with others." ~ **Tom Ford**

You cannot fulfil your Destiny on your own. At one point or another you will need to leverage on experiences, gifts, anointing's, ideas, talents, revelations and insights from other relationships. You cannot be self-sufficient.

Your wisdom will come from your mentors. Your anointing will come from your pastors. Your guidance will come from your counsellors. Your spiritual protection will come from your intercessors and prophetic watchmen that God has assigned for you etc. If you do not value relationships, then many things that you are supposed to lay hold of will never reach you. So, you must understand and embrace the power of agreement and synergy, and remember that resources flow through relationships.

There are relationship codes and rules of engagement that you will learn as you go along. They will assist you greatly in developing and maintaining healthy Destiny relationships (such as knowing that you are an imperfect vessel relating with other imperfect vessels). You will need a lot of wisdom, grace and patience.

"Good relationships don't just happen, they take time, patience and two people who want to be together." ~ **Tiny Buddha**

There are relationships that are so crucial to your Destiny so that when such people purport to reject or ignore you, you must pursue them and cling to them no matter what. Your pride and sentiments must never get in the way of your Destiny and sometimes you must force your loyalty on them where your Destiny depends on them.

It is important that you discern the value and relevance that each relationship is bringing into your life as well as the value and relevance that you yourself are bringing into that relationship. It is also important is for you to discern and ascertain the relationships (that are not your portion that do not add any value or relevance to your Destiny) because they take up valuable time and space in your life.

It is therefore important you learn to let go of all non-value adding relationships so that you can soar higher. This means walking away from dysfunctional and toxic relationships and detaching yourself emotionally from any other relationship that may not be necessarily toxic or dysfunctional, but it is not useful for where you are going.

"All relationships go through hell. Real relationships get through it."
Unknown

It matters who you surround yourself with.

"You are the average of the 5 people you spend the most time with."
Jim Rohn

This is because the people we surround ourselves with, influence our behaviors, habits, values and attitudes etc. (which ultimately sets the course and direction of our lives). The company we keep also impacts and influences our choices and decisions (which ultimately impacts on the quality of our lives. So, surround yourself with those on the same mission as you, those who are pregnant with Destiny like yourself.

- Surround yourself with those who only lift you higher not with those who pull and weigh you down.
- Surround yourself with people who have dreams, desire, and ambition because they will help you push for, and realize your own. If you surround yourself with positive people who build you up, the sky is the limit.
- Surround yourself with the dreamers, and the doers, the believers, the thinkers, but most of all. Surround yourself with

those who see the greatness within you, even when you don't see it yourself.

- Your friends should motivate and inspire you and your circle should be well rounded and supportive. Keep it tight and choose quality over quantity.
"Keep away from people who try to belittle your ambitions, small people always do that, but the really great people make you feel that you too can become great."

- Surround yourself with positive people who believe in your dreams, encourage your ideas, support your ambitions, and bring out the best in you. Do not expect positive changes in your life if you surround yourself with negative people.

- It is interesting how your quality of life improves dramatically when you surround yourself with good intelligent kind-hearted positive loving people.

- Surround yourself with positive successful people and people who are better than you because they will challenge and provoke you to be better. If you're hanging around bad people, they're going to start bringing you down.

- People either inspire you, or they drain you so pick them wisely. Keep people in your life that will change it for the better. Energy is contagious, positive and negative alike. Be forever mindful of what and who you are allowing into your space.

- Develop and establish expressed or implied codes and terms of engagement in each of your relationships (to minimize conflict and relational breaches etc.) Communicate these codes and terms clearly and articulately to all those you are in a relationship with.

Beyond the general principles about relationships, there are other more subtle wisdom nuggets that you will need to adopt when managing your more delicate relationships (especially those that impact directly on your Destiny). These include your relationship with your Destiny midwife and spiritual authority, your Destiny helpers and your Destiny peers, your Destiny assignees, mentees, coaches and spiritual seed, your co-workers and colleagues whether in the church or in the marketplace in whichever sector or sphere of influence you may be operating in.

A relationship becomes a Destiny relationship and a divine connection when it has the power to either enhance or derail your journey to Destiny. To that extent you cannot afford to just walk out of such relationships just because something has gone wrong. You should adopt some of the following wisdom nuggets depending on the situation you are in.

These wisdom nuggets will come to you over time and they will mainly be imparted upon you by your role models or those others who have gone ahead of you and who have left valuable lessons you can learn from.

1. **KNOWING WHEN TO ADOPT STRATEGIC SILENCE AND TACTICAL RETREATS**

One of the things that often plagues many of us women is talking excessively and unnecessarily when engaging with those we are in a relationship with. To that extent you will often encounter a "verbal puncture" and "verbal potholes" when your words become unwholesome, toxic, skewed, offensive, unfiltered, and unguarded. Where your speech contains a hint of woundedness or toxicity and it threatens the health of that relationship you are in.

You must at that point stop your "verbal vehicle" and do a quick damage control.

- A *"verbal vehicle"* refers to your communication.
- *"Verbal puncture"* refers to a breach in that communication.
- *"Verbal potholes"* refer to the root causes that lead to *"verbal punctures"*.

Your ability to realize that you have hit a "verbal pothole" and that you have suffered a "verbal puncture" is crucial in enabling you to do a quick and timely stop gap measure by bandaging the puncture. However, and more importantly is your ability to do a more effective and long-term repair work to that puncture for the sake of that relationship and ultimately for the sake of your Purpose and Destiny.

"Silence isn't empty, its full of answers" Unknown

This will entail you adopting a strategic silence and a tactical retreat where you send yourself on a "verbal exile" and "verbal wilderness" to scan your emotions and thoughts by acknowledging the *"verbal puncture"*. Identifying the root causes. Re-evaluating the damage, it caused. Seeking how to repair and heal it. Then you can safely trust yourself again to return from your verbal wilderness and salvage that relationship.

"Silence is a great source of strength." Unknown

Chances are that the other person in the relationship was also able to discern your "verbal pothole and puncture" so that you are on the same page (when you go on your verbal exile and wilderness) because otherwise that person may be left confused and even deeply wounded by your unilateral "verbal exit". The emergency bandaging of your verbal puncture we talked of earlier, is therefore crucial in ensuring that your connection remains intact, while you embark on the long-term repair work.

However, there are some cautions that you must be aware of before you embark on a strategic silence and a tactical retreat as follows;

- Ensure that the emergency bandaging means apologizing to the other person and expressing regret for your unwholesome speech (so that your strategic silence is clothed with sincere motives and genuine remorse).

- Ensure that you are indeed strategic and tactful, so that the adopting of silence and retreating, does not amount to emotionally forsaking or disconnecting from that relationship.
- Ensure you do not over extend your silence and retreat as it could damage your relationship irreparably. When silence and absence are too long you may subconsciously enter a dangerous comfort zone that may jeopardise and abort that relationship.

To this extent all other dynamics of the relationship should remain intact such as fulfilling your usual roles and obligations in that relationship (while your verbal communication is taking a break). Strategic silence does not mean becoming a mute and it is simply going on a "verbal diet" where you minimize communication and only talk on a need to basis, until your verbal puncture is healed. Your retreating does not mean a total exit, but a wise separating and keeping of distance for a suitable period of time.

Ecclesiastes 3:7 *"There is a time to speak and a time to keep silence"*

2. KNOWING HOW TO DEAL WITH THOSE YOU NO LONGER TRUST

Your relationships no matter how divine they may be, will not always necessarily flow smoothly without any hitches. Being human, there will be portholes and punctures that will cause hitches, frictions, and tensions from time to time (which may not be serious enough to break the relationship) but they will nonetheless have some negative impact which you must address, handle and manage, in order to keep the relationship intact and beneficial.

Once such hitch is a *"trust pothole"* that causes a *"trust puncture"* which must be repaired before you can move on. While ideally every one of your relationships should be based on the titanium pillar of trust, sadly and inevitably that trust may be shaken, eroded and sometimes even uprooted completely due to our human failings, weaknesses and shortcomings. Yet that relationship must go on because obligations and roles must continue to be fulfilled and expectations met for the benefit of your mutual Destinies.

Sometimes it will be you, who will break the trust. When it is the other person who breaks that trust, it is incumbent upon you to adopt this golden wisdom nugget of embracing the grace to deal with that person (who you no longer trust) with caution, redefined boundaries and revised terms of engagement.

This is an extremely delicate balancing act. It will require an amazing grace on your part plus a mature acceptance that this relationship is crucial for the fulfilment of your Destiny and you cannot afford to discard it.

Granted it is very difficult not to trust someone you are dealing regularly with. The temptation is to drop your guard and extend trust again and again (whether consciously or subconsciously) only to get severely betrayed and hurt again because you did not give that person sufficient time to earn and regain your trust.

Your ability to successfully balance this, is an evident sign of your emotional and spiritual maturity which will have developed over time.

However, it is important to keep your heart open when it becomes clear that it is time to trust that person again.

The book "Boundaries" by Pastor Sam Hinn is invaluable in addressing and advising on trust in relationships.

3. KNOWING YOUR VALUE AND RELEVANCE DESPITE YOUR WEAKNESSES

"Know your worth. Know the difference between what you are getting and what you deserve." **Unknown**

Some of the core elements of any Destiny relationship, are the value and relevance you each bring into that relationship.

Value means that there are gifts, skills, talents and human endowments and resources of great worth (within you and within the other person).

Relevance means that your presence in that person's life whether physically, emotionally, financially, spiritually or socially is necessary, useful and important to enhance that person's Destiny. And likewise, that person's presence in your life.

Your recognition and understanding of what value and relevance you each bring to that relationship is crucial to your ability to manifest and release that value and relevance into that relationship.

Having value and relevance does not mean the absence of shortcomings and weaknesses in a person. Likewise having shortcomings and weaknesses does not mean the absence of value and relevance in a person. These elements co-exist within each one of us and it is our responsibility to manage them appropriately.

However, there will be times when our shortcomings and weaknesses are so grossly magnified in a relationship (as a result of certain bad behaviours, habits, and poor choices) that we may experience a confidence crisis.

We may consciously or subconsciously question and doubt our value and relevance in that relationship. This may lead us to undermine and compromise that value and relevance by withdrawing and withholding it to the detriment of the other party and more tragically to the breakdown and death of that relationship.

"No one can determine your value except you. Stop focusing on your self-limiting beliefs. Embrace your self-worth." **Unknown**

4. KNOWING HOW TO BECOME COLLATERAL DAMAGE FOR A GREATER GOAL

Sometimes in the course of accomplishing a task there might be injury, liability or damage that was not desired or intended. This may fall and affect innocent parties and there is nothing anyone can do about it. Sometimes the injury and damage is foreseeable and it cannot be avoided and it will for sure affect certain people. That task will proceed irrespective and certain people become collateral damage.

Contrary to common belief that all relationships should be equal in terms of bargaining power, leverage and commitment, it is not always so when it comes to Destiny relationships. The input by each party may differ in terms of their value and relevance.

So, it is crucial for you to look at each relationship separately and understand its weight and measure (so that you may know how to position yourself).

For example, the relationship between a parent and a child is in itself a Destiny relationship and where the child is still dependent on the parent. It would be very foolish of the child to imagine that he or she has the same bargaining power and weight as the parent. Also, the relationship between a master and servant, a leader and a follower, a sponsor and one being sponsored, or between a spiritual authority and a spiritual son.

It is with this humble revelation in mind that you may find yourself in a situation where you must accept to become collateral damage. To incur the liability, grievance, blame and smear to your reputation. To take a lesser deal than you expected, for the sake of that relationship (after weighing the value of your Destiny vis-à-vis these effects of becoming collateral damage).

A ready example is where you may be serving a leader and something goes wrong in the course of undertaking a task, and someone must take the blame and suffer the consequences. The leader makes it quite clear that he or she cannot afford to be the one. It becomes evident to you that more harm will be done by the leader taking the blame, than you taking the blame. To that extent you become collateral damage and you clearly see the wisdom in doing so in order to safeguard that relationship and your Destiny.

This is a golden wisdom nugget that you must embrace graciously and humbly by keeping your focus on the bigger picture, the greater goal, and the higher rewards that will automatically come.

Becoming collateral damage is a price you have to pay in your journey to Destiny and an important key to navigating your Destiny relationships for maximum benefits.

5. KNOWING WHEN TO HAVE "NO OPINION" IN A MATTER

It is a misconception that being wise and intelligent means that you must have an opinion on everything under the sun. In fact, it is very unwise for you to spew out uninformed and careless opinions on issues that may either not concern you or you have no adequate understanding of.

So sometimes it is better to humbly but boldly refrain.

"The quieter you become the more you are able to hear." **Rumi**

The temptation to offer opinions where you should not, can either be as a result of you trying to meet the unrealistic expectations of others (by responding to pressure and undue duress) or as an attempt to appear knowledgeable and clever.

It is completely in order for you to say that you have "no opinion" on a matter and still be respected so that when you do have an opinion on a matter it will carry more weight and credibility because people have come to trust your judgment.

"There is nothing more classier, than a Woman who stays quiet, because the Holy Spirit has told her not to speak even though she knows the answer" **Harrington**

The possible negative consequence of rushing to give an opinion is that whatever stand you take on an issue (naively, recklessly or with pride) will affect those in your relationships as well as your credibility and integrity and no one wants to deal with a liability.

One way of healing from this malady is to listen more and speak less.

In addition, learning to hold your tongue when you are in the presence of greatness will help you shape and refine your opinions in wisdom.

Once you have a relationship with a person who is obviously wiser and more experienced than you (and from whom you are expected to tap wisdom and knowledge) then it is very short-sighted of you to outtalk that person and be hasty in offering opinions on issues whether solicited or unsolicited and thereby miss the precious and golden opportunity to learn from the experts.

However, having "no opinion" on a matter must be sincere as opposed to an arrogant and irresponsible withholding of information and knowledge that is within your possession, and that you have a responsibility to provide. So, this will require you to walk in wisdom and sincerity.

6. KNOWING HOW TO EXTRACT THE GOOD IN OTHERS AND DISCARD THE REST

Not everything that comes from other people in your relationships is necessary for you. It is therefore important to discern what to take from each person and what to reject, no matter how wise or learned that person may be.

The input you are intended to receive from the people in your relationships is that which is specifically relevant to your Purpose and Destiny. Since those you are receiving it from have a lot in them (whether it be positive or negative), then you must be careful to only receive that which is your portion and overlook anything else that is either not profitable for you or at worst it is detrimental to you.

As agreed earlier we are human beings, we have our flaws weaknesses and shortcomings. It would be suicidal of you to tap and draw everything without sieving it just because that person is wiser, older and more experienced than you.

Sometimes some of the wisest most gifted and most knowledgeable people are also greatly flawed. You must sieve and sift whatever you receive from them (but without throwing out the baby with the bath water so to speak).

It is also worthy to note that those receiving from you are also wise enough to sieve and reject that which is not good for them in you.

7. KNOWING HOW TO CONCEAL YOUR GREATNESS WITH "DIVINE FOOLISHNESS".

It goes without saying that your relationships will not be perfect (despite the fact that they are very crucial and valuable). Sometimes the anointing, gifting, talents, skills, within you, may threaten, irritate and annoy those in your relationships (even though unjustifiably). Some people around you may be undergoing their own frustrations and your greatness is a slap in their face.

In other words, you will ultimately come to the revelation that not everyone can handle your greatness. The golden wisdom nugget here is to avoid flaunting it and instead wisely conceal it with a wise mask of *"divine foolishness"*.

This means that while you and those others who matter know the greatness within you, it is not necessary for everyone to know it or see it (especially if they cannot handle it).

Not everyone with whom you have a divine connection and a Destiny relationship, will like you. Some of them will simply put up with you because they are fulfilling their mandated role and assignment in your life obediently and faithfully. They know that their obedience or disobedience impacts on their own Destiny. So, like the Prophet Elijah who does not appear to have actually liked his protégé Elisha, yet he tolerated him because he knew that he needed Elisha as much as Elisha needed him for each of them to ultimately fulfil and enter their Destiny.

The whole idea, is to safe guard your relationships by managing and navigating them with minimum tension and friction. Learn to wisely and patiently accommodate the weaknesses in those you are relating with, even as they patiently accommodate your weaknesses.

When people who are insecure around you, think or believe that there is nothing so great or special within you, or they fail to see it, then it makes it easier for you to do your thing without any unnecessary friction and disruption. Otherwise, your greatness only attracts negative attention and makes them stumble.

"Divine foolishness" is a golden wisdom nugget whereby you hide your greatness from those who cannot handle it. Instead, you allow them to underestimate you so that you are no longer a threat to them. More importantly where that greatness is still growing (and can be easily crushed and stifled by those who either do not understand it or are offended by it) then you must be wise and walk in *"divine foolishness"*.

This is the wisdom of hiding your hand from your dream killers. For example, according to the bible (1 Samuel 21:13), David was greatly afraid of Achish the king of Gath because he was being recognized by the servants of Achish and they knew what a great warrior David was. This led David to feign insanity and drool like a mad man in order to avoid harm from Achish the king of Gath.

The most important but perhaps also the most disheartening revelation that you will get about some of your Destiny helpers is that no matter how valuable and relevant they are to your Destiny, nonetheless they are still human and there may be episodes when that Destiny helper, may manifest the traits of a Destiny killer (whether intentionally or unintentionally). As a result of any number of reasons. You must learn to wisely manage those episodes by remaining hidden in "divine foolishness" until those episodes pass because for sure they will pass, and those Destiny helpers will take back their rightful roles and assignments over your life.

In summary therefore, learn to hold on stubbornly to your Destiny relationships and to not only survive within those difficult ones but to also thrive and allow them to enhance your journey to Destiny by adopting these wisdom nuggets.

Before you can understand how to deal with your Destiny helpers, Destiny killers, sibling rivals, spice girls and suspect suitors, it is important that you first understand how to relate and have a relationship with yourself. Hence the reason the following chapter addresses knowing yourself and what kind of a Destiny Woman you are.

Destiny Questions to Ponder On

1) *In what other ways can you apply the wisdom of adopting a strategic silence and making a tactful retreat?*

2) *In what other ways can you apply the wisdom of dealing with those you no longer trust?*

3) *In what other ways can you apply the wisdom to own and maintain your value and relevance despite your shortcomings and weaknesses?*

4) *In what other ways can you apply the wisdom to become collateral damage for a greater goal?*

5) *In what other ways can you apply the wisdom of having "no opinion" in a matter?*

6) *In what other ways can you apply the wisdom to sieve and sift what you need and reject the rest?*

7) *In what other ways can you apply the wisdom to conceal your greatness with divine foolishness?*

This Page Was Intentionally Left Blank

Chapter Two

THE PARADOXICAL DESTINY WOMAN

Owning Your Absurdity Without Apology

Chapter Preview

1) **The Leper Within the Giant**

   (When your strengths and weaknesses work in perfect harmony)

2) **The Fountain of Folly Within the Well of Wisdom**

   (When your folly enhances your wisdom)

3) **The Imposter Syndrome Hiding Within Your Greatness**

   (When your greatness accommodates your imposter syndrome)

4) **The Power Within the Pain**

   (When you become a balm for others)

5) **The Thorn Within the Rose**

   (Appreciating your best of times during your worst of times)

6) **The Vessel so Gifted Yet, So Flawed**

   (Your flavor is in your flaws)

7) **The Maidservant Within the Queen**

   (When your humility crowns your power)

INTRODUCTION

You may be the kind of woman whose character contains certain paradoxes. These may confuse others to the point where they even question your sanity. However, a closer scrutiny will reveal that you are indeed a woman of destiny capable of fulfilling that destiny despite these paradoxes. As Charles Caleb Cotton once said, *"A woman is an embodied paradox, a bundle of contradictions."*

The use of the word "paradox" also needs explaining. A paradox is a situation where two things, presented alongside each other in the same person or situation, appear to oppose each other yet, on closer inspection, turn out to be perfectly capable of co-existing in a state of creative tension. On the surface, the co-existence of these two qualities may appear illogical. More careful consideration, however, reveals them to be manifestations of a deeper logic. To say that a woman is an embodied paradox may have been a snipe on the lips of Mister Cotton, but in this chapter, we will see that it is, in fact, her in-built paradoxes that enable this type of woman to overcome obstacles both radically and effectively.

Often women who contain paradoxical qualities may be confused into thinking that there is something wrong with them. Other people may look at them and regard them as confused. In response, such a woman may try to change her paradoxical nature because she either believes or has been told that she needs to align and conform to the norm to be effective and make progress. Sadly, such attempts to change her only throw her into greater confusion, chaos, and ineffectiveness. As a result, she may find herself in a depressive state not knowing what to do. This may continue until she comes to her "aha" moment and realizes she is what she is and that there is nothing wrong with her.

Then she begins to understand herself and embrace her complex and creative nature. Therefore, the real paradox is that these inbuilt paradoxes are in fact the very things that act as a catalyst to make this type of woman able to overcome her obstacles in a deep and lasting way. In the process, contrary to traditional beliefs and standard expectations, she ironically turns out to be a very viable destiny candidate.

It is therefore important for you, as a woman of destiny, to possess a measure of healthy and accurate self-knowledge through which you understand not only your unique qualities, odd traits, strange proclivities, and mysterious idiosyncrasies but also how they either empower or disempower you. This will prevent you from trying to conform to what tradition says a destiny candidate should look like and imploding in the process.

One indisputable fact about a woman with any of these paradoxes is the fact that she may not be a good person in the traditional sense. Indeed, she may have a lot of flaws. At the same time, paradoxically, she has the mark of destiny all over her. She therefore cannot be dismissed so easily. She is a paradox. As Demez White celebrates: "She is a puzzle; she is faithful and yet detached, she is committed and yet relaxed, she loves everyone and yet no one, she is sociable and yet a loner, she's gentle yet tough, she's passionate but can also be platonic/aloof. In short, she is predictable in her unpredictability."

Some of the contradictory traits in this kind of a woman are fascinating. In what follows, I will look at seven.

1. THE LEPER WITHIN THE GIANT

(When your strengths and weaknesses work in perfect harmony)

Thomas Paine once famously remarked:

"I love the man that can smile in trouble, that can gather strength from distress, and grow brave by reflection. 'Tis the business of little minds to shrink, but he whose heart is firm, and whose conscience approves his conduct, will pursue his principles unto death."

While a giant symbolizes power and strength, something that is larger than life, gigantic, something to be feared, a leper symbolizes that which is weak, incapacitated, immobilized and undesirable.

When the qualities of the leper and the giant coexist in the same person, that's what I would call a paradox.

As a woman who is serious and intentional about fulfilling her purpose and destiny, you will often appear like a giant to outsiders. They see you as strong, wise, and well put together. Little do they know that within you is a leper struggling with insecurities, fears and doubts as to whether you really have what it takes to fulfil your purpose and enter your destiny.

This paradox is effective because the giant that is visible to others becomes a great source of encouragement to those struggling to fulfil their own purpose and destiny. Consequently, when such people regard you as a giant from whom they can draw strength and encouragement, let the giant within you emerge. Do not become self-effacing and default to the leprous side of your thinking. This will be counter-productive because:

i.   Those around you cannot see the leper within you
ii. The leper within you does not have the capacity to help them.

There is nothing noble or heroic in trying to show people the weak and worst aspect of you when what those people need to see is the best and the strongest aspects in you. The leper is for your eyes only. The only purpose the leper serves is to keep you humble and realistic regarding those areas within you that are still flawed and in need of work. Anything that hinders the giant from fully manifesting belongs to the inner leper.

Women respond differently to this paradox of the leper and the giant. One woman may completely forget the leper because she allows people's positive perception of her to go to her head and to deceive her that there surely cannot be a leper within her if the only thing people are seeing is the giant. Another woman only sees the inner leper despite people's perspective of her as a giant. She therefore convinces herself that either people are mocking her by seeing her as a giant or they are mistaken in their assessment.

Both these women are wrong.

They need to become a third type of woman - one who is able to balance this paradox by seeing that there is a giant and a leper within her, coexisting with each other, and serving a crucial role in enabling her to fulfil her purpose and destiny, provided she learns how to manifest the giant and manage the leper with excellence.

This ability to manifest the giant and manage the leper comes over time and is the result of a costly process of inner formation. As Demi Lovato says, *"Nothing is more beautiful than the smile that has struggled through tears."*

2. THE FOUNTAIN OF FOLLY WITHIN THE WELL OF WISDOM

(When your folly enhances your wisdom)

Ralph Waldo Emerson once said that *"For every grain of wit, there is a grain of folly."*

Another paradox you will find within you is the combination of two apparently contradictory qualities: firstly, the ability to be a deep well, source, and reservoir of wisdom in handling other people's matters - in guiding, mentoring, coaching counselling, or just encouraging and edifying others. This wisdom empowers you to walk with them through difficult situations - whether business, careers, and relationships - and to offer unprecedented wisdom and insight that propels them into success and victory.

Secondly, when it comes to your own business, career, or relationships, you find that you have this strange ability to drink from the fountain of folly. Once you have quaffed its water, you find yourself going round in circles while you watch those you have satisfied from your well of wisdom leave you behind!

This paradox seems to serve three purposes.

i. It reveals that there is indeed a well of wisdom within you because you can clearly see the tangible evidence in the lives of those you advise
ii. The fountain of folly reminds you that you still don't know it all and that you need to consult with other senior and more experienced individuals and drink from their wells of wisdom even as others drink from yours
iii. This causes you to remain thirsty for greater and deeper wisdom lest you imagine that you are self-sufficient and all-knowing. You must therefore surround yourself with those whose wells of wisdom are deeper than your own.

Women respond differently to this paradox. One woman will focus on the well of wisdom and completely deny the fountain of folly. This denial is likely to dry up the well of wisdom because, interestingly, it is the presence of the fountain of folly that makes you see the need to keep refilling the well of wisdom.

Another woman will focus more on the fountain of folly within her and deny the presence of the well of wisdom because she can't grasp how the two can coexist. She therefore allows the well of wisdom to dry up because she fails to use or refill it. She fails to quench people's need for wisdom because she doesn't believe she has any such resource within her.

Both women are wrong.

A third kind of woman is needed – one whose response is balanced. She understands and embraces both the well of wisdom and the fountain of folly as well as the crucial role each plays in empowering her to fulfil her purpose and destiny.

3. THE IMPOSTER SYNDROME HIDING WITHIN YOUR GREATNESS

(When your greatness accommodates your imposter syndrome)

An imposter is a person who pretends to be someone or something else to deceive others, especially for fraudulent gain or higher social status. An imposter syndrome is when you regard yourself as an imposter. It derives from a belief that your success is not deserved or has not been legitimately achieved with your own efforts and skills. In other words, an imposter syndrome is an act of undermining the greatness within you. "Greatness" is the state of being great (as in size, skill, achievement, power, success, distinction, prominence, and significance). As Tina Fey comments, *"The beauty of the impostor syndrome is you vacillate between extreme egomania and a complete feeling of 'I'm a fraud! Oh God, they're on to me! I'm a fraud'!"*

One of the most interesting paradoxes for a woman of destiny is that even when you know there is some greatness within you (manifesting itself in accomplishments, successes and victories in your journey to destiny), you still doubt that you are the one who has attained these triumphs. Even where you do believe that you have conquered some challenge, you somehow wonder whether you did so legitimately - whether you faked it by conning your way towards your successes. This is often because your attainments came in adversity and you did not realize that you were miraculously thriving in the worst seasons of your life.

If you're a woman with an imposter syndrome, you will feel nervous and embarrassed when you receive accolades and praises because you imagine people can see through you and that what they are looking at is a person who doesn't deserve such applause.

Does this imposter syndrome therefore ever serve a useful purpose? Yes, provided you manage it and balance it with your greatness. The simple fact that you are questioning whether and how you accomplished these things leads you to a humble acknowledgment that it was by God's grace that you triumphed, as well as through the assistance of many people who enabled you to arrive where you are now. Once you come to that revelation and appreciate those people, you will stop feeling like an imposter and humbly and graciously celebrate yourself. Your greatness will shine legitimately, without any shadow of doubt.

The danger of not balancing your greatness and your imposter syndrome is that you will either develop an exaggerated sense of self-importance or develop a crippling sense of self-doubt and shame. Both this inflated sense of ego and that debilitating feeling of unworthiness will hinder your ability to fulfil your destiny.

Emma Watson, the Hollywood actress, says this. *"When I was younger, I just did it. I just acted. It was just there. So now, when I receive recognition for my acting, I feel incredibly uncomfortable. I tend to turn in on myself. I feel like an impostor. It was just something I did."*

Remember this: people can make you feel like an imposter; when they constantly undermine your greatness, they make you believe that you are nothing. If you believe their lies, you walk around feeling like a fraud even when you are truly thriving, when your authentic and merited greatness is truly on display.

As a woman possessing this paradox you must ignore those who constantly attempt to devalue, belittle, and undermine the greatness within you. Some of them will do this out of a sincere misunderstanding because they become focused on what they perceive to be your flaws and blind to the greatness within you. Others will undermine you out of envy because they cannot handle your greatness because it somehow threatens them.

Your strategy is to adopt a "divine foolishness." Confident in who you are, you allow others to see only your flaws so that your greatness remains concealed from them. That way, you silence their attempts to kill the greatness within you. Your greatness will then continue to have an impact - perhaps even more powerfully without it being dramatically visible - and your detractors and critics will then get a shock when they finally realize the immense progress you have made in your "divine foolishness".

4. THE POWER WITHIN THE PAIN

(When you become a balm for others)

Another amazing paradox which you may find within you is the capacity to continue in your leadership role effectively and fruitfully even while you are suffering great pain from issues in your own life. As a leader, you do not have the luxury of allowing this pain to stand in the way of your leadership role as you fulfil your purpose and destiny.

Even more paradoxical is the fact that while you are still hurting you are simultaneously releasing tremendous healing to those you lead. This is because you have come to a level of maturity whereby you know how to sieve and sift the negative, wounded, unhealthy emotions within you so that you only exhibit and release those emotions that are productive and beneficial to the people you are leading. While hurting leaders often end up hurting people, you do the opposite, hence the paradox.

This wounded warrior contains strength and weakness all wrapped up together. In your woundedness, you can be hurting deeply but you manage to comfort and console another person (who is not aware of your pain) and you release deep healing to them.

This is paradoxical!

This seemingly contradictory ability to turn your pain into power, your bleeding into balm, your wounds into wisdom, teaches you that there is a healing power within your suffering. You should embrace both pain and power and allow them to coexist until you receive your own healing. More importantly, while they are coexisting within you, you should not hesitate to continue healing others while you are hurting.

Fortunately, your Paradoxical nature makes it easy for you to balance your hurting self and your healing of others by embracing your pain instead of denying it. You suspend your focus on it long enough to focus instead on healing others.

5. THE THORN WITHIN THE ROSE

(Appreciating your best of times during your worst of times)

Anne Bronte once said, "He that dares not grasp the thorn should never crave the rose." This rose-and-thorn paradox depicts something painfully beautiful and something beautifully painful - a piercing fragrance, a beautiful pain, a flawed beauty. Thorns humble the rose because without them the flower might become haughty and proud because of its magnificent beauty and extraordinary fragrance. The rose beautifies the thorns because without it, there would only be a wasteland of briers and barrenness.

What is your thorn and why is it there? The fact that thorns weaken us to strengthen us is a paradox. As a woman of destiny, you will inevitably experience a thorn or thorns in your flesh. These symbolize irritations, aggravations, sufferings, torments, sorrows, afflictions. Your roses symbolize gifts, talents, beauty, achievements.

As a Paradoxical Woman you will contain and combine both roses and thorns in your personality. There will be a sweet and fragrant side of you and a prickly side too. This odd combination may confuse many people. Suffice to say that you understand the role and purpose of your sweet and fragrant side and the role and purpose of your prickly side - that together they work interdependently to enhance you for destiny.

The relationship between roses and thorns traverses the line between sweetness, beauty, and love on the one hand (roses), and the pangs of hardship, unexpected loss, and pain on the other (thorns). After you have struggled with these thorns for some time, you may seek to eliminate them from your life because of a misguided notion that you cannot fulfil your destiny unless your life is a path strewn only with roses. This is a mistake; you fulfil your destiny because of, and in spite of, the thorns. Your ability to endure the thorny seasons is crucial. You must learn to smell the roses when the thorns are out to destroy or derail you. Your strategy should be to give so much value and priority to your destiny, and to be so passionate about fulfilling it, that the thorns in your life pale into insignificance in comparison to the benefits of fulfilling your destiny. It is the roses that give you the strength to endure the thorns and it is the thorns that give you the ability to appreciate the roses. As Olga Broumas says, *"She who loves roses must be patient and not cry out when she is pierced by thorns."*

Every rose has its thorns and this teaches us an important truth about human nature too: namely, that nobody is perfect and that even the most beautiful situations have an ugly side to them, and every ugly situation has a beautiful aspect to it somewhere. The statement, "he who has a rose must respect the thorn," teaches us that in relationships you should not expect people to be perfect; even good people have flaws. It is often said that from the thorn comes a rose and from the rose comes the thorn. Sometimes something can appear at the start to be unattractive because all we can see are flaws, but it can grow to look beautiful in time so we should not dismiss thorny situations or people too quickly. Who knows what roses may come from them when we give them time?

Roses and thorns demonstrate the interconnection between beauty and ugliness, joy and sadness, glory and suffering. Whenever we try to make sense of suffering by looking for the purpose in our pain, it is the fragrant presence of the roses in the prickly seasons of our discomfort that brings us the consolation we need to persevere.

Perhaps the most admirable quality about the paradoxical connection between a rose and a thorn is the fact that thorns arouse us from our comfort zones so that whatever has been dormant in our lives can grow to empower us in the journey to destiny. In the process, the beauty and fragrance of the roses make that painful growth bearable. As women of destiny, we must accept thorny struggles and allow the thorns to teach us powerful lessons if we are to become vessels of strength and honour.

The crown of thorns that Jesus was forced to wear when he was being crucified symbolized mockery and degradation, yet, at the end of it all, you and I receive the roses of life and redemption through those thorns. In other words, our redemption, deliverance, healing, blessings, and salvation were roses hidden within the thorns of the crown that Jesus wore when he was being crucified.

Sometimes you may find yourself going through a very traumatic and stressful season in one area of your life - such as in your business, where you are facing a financial collapse and bankruptcy from which you can't even imagine that you will ever recover. In addition, that devastation comes with serious repercussions for your reputation and integrity, throwing you off balance in fear, pain, and anguish. Yet, at the same time in another area of your life, you are experiencing the greatest joy possible - for example, in the miraculous healing of a loved one who for sure you thought was a lost cause. You may be encountering the ugliest problems and yet find yourself in the beautiful landscape of miracles.

There are different responses to this kind of paradox. You may focus so much on the ugly problem and completely fail to see the beauty and the joy from the health solution. In the process, you fail to be grateful and this may affect some of those around you very negatively. Likewise, you may choose to focus on the beauty and the joy and completely deny the ugly problem. You then fail to take necessary and urgent action to damage control your ugly financial problem, thereby making it worse.

The right, balanced response is for you to embrace the paradox of the two situations and even use the beauty in the healing miracle to ease the pain of your ugly problem, thereby working your favour against your famine. The purpose of the ugly problem in your life is to deal with some aspects of your character, attitude, and heart condition, thereby bringing out patience, endurance, and perseverance, helping you in your onward journey to destiny.

6. THE VESSEL SO GIFTED YET SO FLAWED

(Your flavor is in your flaws)

"We are flawed creatures, all of us. Some of us think that means we should fix our flaws. But get rid of my flaws and there would be no one left." ~ **Sarah Vowell**

One of the most fundamental trademarks of a real woman of destiny is the fact that she is usually so exceptionally gifted, yet at the same time so exceptionally flawed, that to an outsider she appears to be totally disqualified to be a candidate for destiny. However, it is her flaws that cause her to remain supernaturally alert because she knows she has so much working against her. Her strategy is to feed her giftedness so that once it is unleashed to its maximum it will totally intimidate her flaws into submission and oblivion. This woman knows that in the words of Ifeanyi Onuoha, "We are treasure chests with more jewels inside than we can imagine."

Ironically, it is the woman with few flaws who often misses her destiny. She mistakenly feels that she is okay with her sufficient measure of perfection. This causes her not to be alert and not to exert too much effort on her journey; she ends up doing the bare minimum because she foolishly settles for what she has. She forgets what Erin Hunter teaches, that "We all have our flaws. But we overcome them. And sometimes, it's our flaws that make us who we are." Our treasure is hidden in earthen vessels; we are weak, frail, fragile, yet God works through us, that way know that it is through Him that we excel.

A phenomenally gifted and flawed woman is precious treasure in a very ugly wrapping. People will write her off and dismiss her because of her appearance. They will fail to discover the treasure within. They miss the paradox that someone so strong and powerful in so many areas of her life can be so weak in another area. Samson could tear a full-grown lion with his bare hands, yet he was so weak that he fell for the wiles of a non-descript and insignificant Delilah. A woman of destiny lives in the same paradox.

7. THE MAIDSERVANT WITHIN THE QUEEN

(When your humility crowns your power)

Robert Greenleaf writes that "good leaders must first become good servants." It is an admirable ability to balance power with humility. On the one hand, the queenly qualities within you make you aware of your power, position, influence, and affluence. You have confidence, you are knowledgeable, you are equipped and empowered for your assignment. There are those under you willing to learn from you because they respect you and are submitted to you. You have a burden for your people, and you understand your responsibilities. Therefore, many people look up to you for solutions, guidance, and leadership. As the Norwegian proverb says, *"In every woman there is a queen; speak to the queen within you and she will answer."*

On the other hand, it is the qualities of the maidservant within you that mean you are respectful and teachable, aware that you are submitted to the power and instructions of another whom you are serving. The merging of the queen and the maidservant within you is another paradox. Achieving your destiny will in part depend upon your ability to walk in these two diverse identities effectively and beautifully.

A queen has a healthy ego which is necessary for her to get ahead. She is charismatic, noble, and even overbearing at times, yet she can embrace and appreciate the role of others and the need to collaborate. She therefore works well both solo and in groups, even though she appears in control and capable on her own.

The paradox here is the fact that she has a humble heart and is sensitive and receptive to the burdens of her people. She has a great capacity to serve others; she has a true servant's heart which is why I refer to the maidservant nature within her. She obeys the call made by Benjamin Franklin: "Let thy maidservant be faithful, strong and homely." She recognizes and appreciates the capabilities in others, yet her self-confident nature does make her look haughty. This paradox is what gives her the ability to embody the authoritative presence of a queen and at the same time to adopt the demure meekness of a maid in service, where necessary. The queen in her makes her empathetic towards others and sensitive to their needs. As someone once wrote, *"Real queens fix each other's crowns."*

For those looking in from the outside, when they see this type of woman in her maidservant mode and then see her in her queen mode, they cannot believe they are looking at the same woman. They may either conclude that she is hypocritical or extremely weird. They need to remember what someone else once wrote: *"A queen on her throne is a woman who has mastered herself. She's not perfect, but she is complete. She has come to the full realization that everything she needs to fulfil her mission can be found within. She has uncovered her powers and she knows how to use them. She's no longer on the path – she is the path."*

A Paradoxical Woman therefore has the qualities of both a queen and a maidservant and her ability to combine and use these diverse qualities wisely in fulfilling her destiny is what gives her that extra edge.

Whatever paradox is within you, whether it be the leper within the giant, the fountain of folly within the well of wisdom, the imposter syndrome hiding in your greatness, the power within the pain, the thorn within the rose, the perfect vessel with deep flaws and the maidservant within the queen suffice to say these paradoxes do not disqualify you for Destiny, instead they give you an extra edge to forge on and lay hold of your Destiny. So, you should learn to own these paradoxes and make them work in your favour.

Destiny Questions to Ponder

1. *What do you sense most within you - the leper or the giant?*

2. *In what ways do you think you can drain your fountain of folly so that your well of wisdom can overflow?*

3. *How can you ensure that the imposter syndrome does not completely suffocate the greatness within you?*

4. *How long can you continue to lead while bleeding or heal while hurting? Is there a time when your bleeding starts to stain those you lead?*

5. *How have the roses in your life helped you cope with the thorns?*

6. *What flaws have you noticed within you and how have they affected your ability to fulfil your destiny?*

7. *How well do you balance your queen qualities and maidservant qualities?*

This Page Was Intentionally Left Blank

Chapter Three

THE DESTINY HELPERS OF A VISION BEARER

Nurturing the Relationships that

Propel You to Destiny

Chapter Preview

1. *Your Destiny Burden Bearers*

2. *Your Destiny Gifted Guild*

3. *Your Destiny Ladder Holders*

4. *Your Destiny Midwives and Leaders*

5. *Your Destiny Mentors, Coaches and Role Models*

6. *Your Destiny Gate Keepers*

7. *Your Destiny Spouse and Family*

OPENING REMARKS

"A Destiny helper is that person or persons divinely created to help you become the person you were created you to be." **Unknown**

Key among the relationships that you will need in your journey to Destiny is that of Destiny helpers. These are people who are sent and ordained to come into your life and aid your path to fulfilment of your Purpose. It will be your responsibility to discern, identify and recognize these relationships that you will encounter and discern the benefit that they are adding to you and to the fulfilment of your Purpose.

Many of your Destiny helpers may not even realize that they are helping you fulfil your Destiny, because they are simply reaching out to do the right thing (like the daughter of Pharaoh when she salvaged the baby Moses from the water, she had no idea that she had preserved him for a great Destiny).

You will of course need to pray and ask God to bring such relationships your way and to also help you relate with them appropriately. Destiny helpers are crucial divine connections that you cannot afford to treat and handle casually or carelessly. You must value them and embrace them and do not disconnect from them until they have accomplished their God-given assignments in your life. One of the most tragic mistakes we often make in our misguided attempts to be strong independent super women, is to disqualify ourselves for assistance. Seeking and getting help does not portray weakness, it portrays maturity.

"The biggest help God can ever give you is the help of knowing who your Destiny helpers are, and you not losing them no matter what."
~ **Unknown**

Firstly, among your Destiny helpers, there will be your burden bearers, your ladder holders, your gifted guild, your Destiny midwife, your mentors, coaches, role models, your gate keepers, your connectors, your sponsors, your protégé's and assignees.

Secondly, among your Destiny helpers there will also be those who don't intend to actually help you. In actual fact their intentions are to discourage and derail you, but unknown to them, your mature response to their negative actions actually ends provoking and propelling you into fulfilling your Purpose and Destiny. To that extent, these relationships (that initially start off negative), end up being very positive and useful.

These are your **Destiny Provokers.**

They include the mediocres (people who may sincerely love you) who have the audacity to suggest to you that you should settle for less than your real Purpose and Destiny.

Your response to mediocres is to ignore them without getting confrontational because chances are they do not yet have a revelation of your Purpose and Destiny and that is the reason they do not understand your zeal and passion for it. They basically seek to discourage you from a point of ignorance. It is actually their ignorant audacity in suggesting that you should settle for less that provokes you into pursuing your Destiny even harder.

"Don't waste your life. No one chooses mediocrity, but many settle. Never settle." ~ **Unknown**

These Destiny Provokers also include mockers, those who taunt you when you are in your barren dry seasons. Their mockery provokes you and pushes you to the place and to the people where your barrenness will be broken.

Your response to the mockers is to make sure that you do not waste any time confronting them or avenging yourself because a mocker does not have the power to break your barrenness. You should instead use your energy and time to focus on those people who do have the power and ability to break your barrenness.

"Mockers will mock you, criticizers will criticize you, condemners will condemn you; don't take it personally; it's their problem not yours." ~ **Unknown**

Yet another category of Destiny helpers are motivators, high achievers, healthy competitors and your own peers etc. whose zeal and passion for their own Purpose makes your own zeal and passion to be ignited towards your own Purpose. As a consequence, we are able to arise from any apathy and continue pursuing our Destiny.

"Competition motivates and drives people to excel, and enables people to learn and benefit from their strengths and weaknesses." **Dr. T.P Chiagant**

Each of these persons and relationships are ordained and designed to usher you and propel you to your Destiny.

It is important to also remain alert and sensitive as to whether a particular Destiny helper is in your life forever or seasonally so that you can manage your transition when the time comes. Also note that premature disconnecting from any of your Destiny helpers can cause irreparable damage to your Destiny where that helper has not exhausted the assignment they have over your life.

Your Destiny helpers add value and they speed up your achievements. When asking God for them, you must have the right motives and the right revelation as to their purpose in your life.

Your Destiny helpers may also include:

- Lifetime Destiny helpers; these are the ones who are in your life to stay from the beginning to the end and their assignments in your life differ from one to the other and they are the ones who add the most value.

- Seasonal Destiny helpers; these are the ones who come in for a particular season to fulfil a particular specific assignment in your life. You must be careful that you do not hold on to them emotionally when their season is over.

- Unstable and erratic Destiny helpers; those who are undergoing their own dysfunctions so they keep stepping in and out of your life, connecting and disconnecting with you. Suffice to say that the moments they do step into your life they add a lot of value. The way to respond to this kind of Destiny helper is to accommodate and be tolerant with their weaknesses and struggles and appreciate the moments when they add value to you. Be careful and be alert so that if they begin to become a liability and a threat to your Destiny, then you must cut them off gently and sensitively until such time as they become stable and consistent again.

Your duty is to pray that every one of your Destiny helpers appears and locates you. That they will have the strength, wisdom, diligence, commitment, and obedience to finish their assignments over your life.

That you will have favour with them and a good relationship. More importantly that they will not become controlling or manipulative, misinterpret and misunderstand their assignments over your life of become distracted with broken focus etc. You must also pray for their protection and against attacks that may come against them from your Destiny killers.

As you fulfil your Purpose and Destiny, with the help of your Destiny helpers, you will also be expected to be a Destiny helper to others. So, you must be alert and sensitive to discern those who approach you expressing their desire for you to either mentor them, hold their ladder as they climb to the top, bear their burdens, midwife them or help them to birth out their Purpose and potential etc.

The first step is to discern that indeed that person is your portion and assignee, by checking if you have the skills set gifting required to help them.

The next step, once you ascertain that you do, is to ascertain through prayer, discernment and insight whether the person is your fit and whether this is the timing for that assignment.

Your role is to provide guidance, motivation, emotional support, role modelling, empower by sharing skills, knowledge and expertise etc.

The biggest challenge you may have is giving your time to others while navigating your own Destiny (especially during trying times), but you must remember that others have given up their time for you and that God intended service to be a two way street of reciprocity, teaching us to assist as we are assisted.

Part of your legacy will be the people that you nurture and usher to their Destiny.

"Your Destiny is fulfilled when you invest in the destinies of others."
~ **Unknown**

1. YOUR DESTINY BURDEN BEARERS

"In a world full of unlimited choices adore those who go hard for you, commitment is a very rare thing." ~ **Unknown**

A burden is a load, a heaviness whether physical, mental, emotional, financial, family, social or spiritual etc. It is something that has to carried or borne with difficulty (including sorrows and troubles, obligations and responsibilities). It could be relational burdens, parental burdens, the burdens of decision making, and the responsibilities you have over all those under your care etc. including the burden of fulfilling your Purpose and Destiny.

Galatians 6:2 *"Bear one another's burdens, and so fulfil the law of Christ."*

Burden bearers are also your inner circle, those who feel your heart beat and can discern the burdens that you are carrying. Their Purpose is to help you bear those burdens and to also offload you off those burdens whether physically, mentally or emotionally. They hear you out as you share deep and intimate aspects of your Vision and the challenges you are encountering (which they cannot share with the other team members) concerning your Vision and Destiny and they can give you wise counsel respectfully and lovingly.

"You are not a burden but you have a burden, which by definition is too heavy to carry on your own." ~ **Unknown**

These are a core group of people released into your life to help you carry your burdens when the load to your Destiny becomes too heavy. They execute and implement your Vision, they oversee your structures and systems, they intercede for you because they are sensitive of your pain so they stand in the gap even when you cannot pray for yourself.

1 Thessalonians 5:11 – *"Therefore comfort each other and edify one another, just as you also are doing."*

These burden bearers who are also your inner circle are:

- People that believe in your big audacious dreams
- People that do not allow you to settle for the status quo
- People that do not want you to follow the crowd but to be your own person.
- People that will not judge your past but will sow in to your future.
- People that will push you to greatness.
- People that will celebrate your success and help you put your failures into perspective.

The characteristics of your burden bearers will be selflessness, generosity, compassion, empathy, strength, wisdom, confidentiality, trustworthy, accountable, reliable and dependable, sensitive and alert, available in and out of season with a servant's heart.

They have a gift and an art for burden bearing and most importantly they have a revelation, a weight and a witness in their heart and spirit of the Call upon your life and its importance so it gives them the motivation to remain committed to you.

The roles of burden bearers include but are not limited to the following:

- Intercessory prayers whereby they bring your burdens to the cross.
- Solving problems and finding solutions for dilemmas
- Executing and implementing tasks, shielding and covering you from unnecessary anxieties and worries.
- To feel your pain which means they lift that pain from off of you and bear it themselves.

"Look out for those who look out for you. Loyalty is everything." ~ **Conor McGregor**

Your Burden Bearers are the people you can really lean on in times of trouble as you fight your anxieties, fears and worries, these are your confidants to whom you can pour out yourself and to whom you can vent and release anything toxic within you that needs to be released for you to move on.

Beyond those of your burden bearers who form your inner circle there will be another category of burden bearers who may not form part of the inner circle but they are nonetheless valuable in bearing your burdens. They are loyal, faithful followers who stick with you till you accomplish your Purpose, they are trusted relationships you can count on in times of trouble, they are there with you when everybody else leaves. They include your members, subscribers, co-workers and labourers and partners in your Vision or project, whether as volunteers or paid workers.

These are your hard-liner supporters like disciples who remain with you and near you in good times and bad times and in every season of your life.

These are also your able assistants, people assigned to bear the burdens that may be weighing you down and hindering you from being effective. Once they discern those burdens, they bear them on your behalf and free you to focus on your Vision.

"Choose people who lift you up." ~ **Michelle Obama**

Burden bearers are your encouragers, edifiers, up lifters who affirm and endorse you because they admire you and what you have been called to do, they cheer you on, championing your course, defending and protecting you where necessary.

"Be an encourager; the world is full of critics already." ~ **Dave Willis**

Burden bearers can be in any area of your life whether in your family life, career and work place, church, corporate sector, business etc. Suffice to say that their roles, mandates and duties will be basically the same, in any of those areas, (namely to offload you, encourage you, edify you and uplift you etc.)

Remember that you are also a burden bearer in somebody else's Vision and Destiny, where you will accord and extend these same services to those whose burdens you are bearing.

Sometimes your inner circle of burden bearers may get too familiar with you or they may forget to draw the boundaries of respect and honour (because they know too much about you and your weaknesses) and they may either knowingly or unknowingly start controlling you or manipulating you. This is not acceptable because their Purpose is to "help" and they must remember that you are still the Vision bearer and they are the Vision helpers so they cannot cross the line and start dictating to you. The minute you discern this toxic situation you must wisely deal with it and if they do not align to their proper role and mandate you must unfortunately begin to cut off such burden bearers before they derail you and your Vision.

2. YOUR DESTINY GIFTED GUILD

These are a group of helpers who are highly skillful in their chosen professions with specific talents and gifts, and expertise (like accountants, lawyers, architects, engineers, singers, artists, musicians, house helpers). These are specialized staff members with specific skills and expertise in certain areas etc. When they come into your life, they use their gifts, talents and skills and expertise to help you accomplish the Purpose for your life.

"People's Purpose in life is always connected to their giftedness." ~ **John C. Maxwell**

These supporters and helpers will join you at various points of your journey and they will have a revelation of what role and assignment they have been ordained to play in your life. As each position themselves correctly, together they will propel you to your Destiny. They are aware that in supporting and helping you fulfil your Destiny, you are also equipping and empowering them to fulfil theirs, so their duty is to usher you and ensure that you have entered your Destiny even as they enter their own.

These gifted and skilled helpers may do so as volunteers or as paid workers. Whether they are volunteers or paid workers the important thing to check is that they have some revelation about your Call and Vision and that they are definitely passionate and sold out to your Vision. They are invested physically, emotionally and mentally, so that for them, it is not just another chore or job, but something they sincerely believe in.

Whether this gifted guild is aware or not, their contribution into your Destiny is not in vain because in the process of them inputting their time, energy skills and expertise into your life, they receive an impartation from you of the gifts, talents, endowments and anointing that are within you, so that as they benefit you, you benefit them.

In the Bible, we find a band of men who had been distressed debtors following David in the wilderness. They discerned that there was greatness within David and that by aligning with him and helping him, they would also get empowered. It is important to notice that when they first joined David, they really had nothing to offer David and they were more of a burden than a blessing, but David did not reject them and instead allowed them in. They began to become empowered by following David until a time came when they became a real help and support for David.

1 Samuel 22:2 – *"And everyone who was in distress, everyone who was in debt, and everyone who was discontented gathered to him. So, he became captain over them. And there were about four hundred men with him."*

Ultimately after they had ushered David to his Destiny, they themselves then entered their own destinies when they were transformed from "distressed debtors" to the "mighty men" of David in his inner leadership. The lesson here is that as a David, you must never despise those sent to follow you (on the grounds that they are initially dependent on you as burdens and as needy mentees). You must never despise a person that has been sent by God to follow and serve you because of their status.

Your connection with those people will be mutually beneficially later on.

1 Chronicles 12:1 – *Now these were the men who came to David at Ziklag while he was still a fugitive from Saul the son of Kish; and they were among the mighty men, helpers in the war,*

3. YOUR DESTINY LADDER HOLDERS

"Those who hold the ladder control the ascent of the leader." ~ **Unknown**

Ladder holders are people who keep you grounded in your values and principles whilst you are fulfilling your Purpose and Destiny. They are the relationships who help you focus on your assignment when everyone is saying you have arrived. They make sure you don't deviate from your assignment; they keep you accountable with constant reality checks.

The reason why someone holds your ladder as you scale the heights is so that you climb steadily and safely, consistently without wavering or falling.

The ladder holder determines the height to which the ladder climber reaches meaning how high the success and Destiny of the climber will be.

When you are climbing the ladder of Destiny to the top, you will need ladder holders to hold your ladder steady as you work to achieve great things. Ladder holders know where you are coming from and where you are going so, they will keep reminding you of your goals. They will promote you and your Visions and dreams, sell your Vision and help other people understand and embrace what it is all about.

"Only surround yourself only with people who are going to take you higher." ~ **Oprah Winfrey**

Your ladder holders believe in you and your Vision and they desire your progress while ensuring to keep your Vision and Purpose relevant and on track without any deviations or distortion.

Who is holding your ladder and whose ladder are you holding because to the same extent you must be somebody else's ladder holder.

The qualities of a good ladder holder is that they are dependable and reliable so that they don't need to be constantly reminded of their obligations. They are intentional and focused and not casual.

They are committed so that they are not holding your ladder while they are looking elsewhere for the next ladder to hold. They should be looking up at you climbing the ladder. They are positive people, not grumblers, and they actually deliver not just offering lip service. They have the required mental and emotional strength, attentiveness, faithfulness, firmness and loyalty so that they are not easily swayed by opinions of other people.

Your may have ladder holders in various areas of your life like your family, your church, your career, business enterprise and in your corporate organization and other institutions because all those areas in your life are related to the Destiny you are fulfilling.

4. YOUR DESTINY MIDWIVES AND LEADERS

Some of the leaders and authorities in your life (whether in your family, society, church, business enterprises, work place, Government, corporate sector) include your parents, your pastors, your elders, your investors and business mentors, employers and bosses. Your political leaders or career mentors and coaches. All are carriers of certain "mantles" necessary for your Destiny.

Mantles are coverings of special empowerment that will enable you to excel and succeed in the various areas of your life and they are released upon you by such authorities and leaders. They are batons passed on through succession in families, business empires, spiritual ministries, corporate bodies, political leadership etc.

In whichever area it is, those leaders and authorities will release a specific type of mantle to empower you.

For example, in the church your pastors and spiritual leaders are gifts to the body of Christ and when you believe in God, you shall be established and when you believe in His prophets and you shall prosper. Your encounter with such servants of God is an encounter with the mind of God, because they are vessels in God's hands for your benefit as your Destiny helpers.

In the business area your leaders there will release business acumen and entrepreneurial skills, your employers and bosses will release an empowerment upon you to own your own enterprise and become a productive employer and boss. In your family, your parents will release an ability to birth and rear healthy families.

In your society the elders there will release an ability to nurture healthy communities. In the political arena your mentors there will release gifts in leadership, and in the corporate area your heads and leaders there will release an empowerment to climb up the corporate ladder.

Therefore, remaining connected and submitted to these leaders and authorities will enable you to tap into the "richness" within them for fulfilling your Purpose and Destiny.

Among these leaders and authorities is another very important relationship namely your "Destiny Midwife" who knows the Calling and Destiny you are carrying within you and they can discern when you conceive it and they know when you should birth it. They help you to birth it and teach you how to nurture it.

"A midwife must possess the hand of a lady, the eyes of a hawk and the heart of a lion." **Aristotle**

The qualities of a good Destiny midwife are the same as those of a natural midwife who helps deliver a natural baby. They are mature, experienced, proactive and calm with a lot of emotional and mental strength, insight, discernment and wisdom. They are your cover, waging warfare against the enemies of your Destiny.

Your Destiny midwife is one who plays a helpful role in bringing forth new power, faith and new beginnings out of you, one who helps produce or bring forth something new. They invest in helping us labour and birth out what is inside us and to push out our gifts, talents, dreams, Visions etc.

Our Destiny midwives plant seeds of faith and words of encouragement and spur us on, helping us not to abort or miscarry our seed. They know how to coach us during the labour pains and birth pangs (not by taking away the pain) by teaching us how to cope and endure until we safely deliver that which we have been carrying, namely our Calling and Destiny.

So, one of the most important Destiny helpers you will encounter in your journey of Destiny will be your midwife. One who will have been ordained to guide you along the way, who will appear in your every season as a teacher and a trainer. When the time comes to birth your Purpose and Destiny this midwife will be there to teach you how to push it out.

Your Destiny midwife has the skills, wisdom and knowledge to know how to pull out your Destiny without killing it. She knows the right circumstances and the perfect timing to ignite and sharpen your gifts and talents, to unleash your potential and help you birth your Purpose and Destiny.

This is because pulling out your Calling before time could kill it and bringing forth your Calling under the wrong circumstances or atmosphere could defile it.

Your response towards your Destiny midwife is to remain submissive, teachable and respectful. Trust and obey instructions faithfully acknowledging that she has been where you have not been and knows what you do not know. As and when you fulfil your Purpose and Destiny, do not forget your midwife who was instrumental in getting you there.

Your Destiny midwife will cover you with prayers and wise counsel to protect you from aborting your Destiny and to equip you with wisdom and tools to enable you to accomplish your Purpose.

Genesis 35:17 – *"Now it came to pass, when she was in hard labour, that the midwife said to her "do not fear; you will have this son also."*

Just like you will need a Destiny midwife to birth your Purpose and Destiny, you will also find that you are a midwife to others that have been assigned to you. You will use the same skills, wisdom, love and care on those people.

"The greatest privilege of a human life is to become a midwife to the awakening of a soul in another person." ~ **Plato**

The greatest mistake you can make is to disconnect prematurely from these Destiny midwives' leaders and authorities for whatever reasons. You could deny yourself crucial help in knowing what you are carrying, when and how to bring it forth in whichever area of your life. The danger is you could have an abortion or miscarriage of Purpose which will prejudice your Destiny.

5. YOUR DESTINY MENTORS, COACHES AND ROLE MODELS

Some of the most needful Destiny helpers for a Destiny Woman in the market place are mentors, coaches and role models. It is important that you actively and intentionally seek out your mentors, coaches and role models that you will need for the various areas of your life and connect yourself to them. Adopting the right protocol so that you earn their favour and acceptance and their willingness to bring you under their wings. You must approach them with humility as opposed to an attitude of entitlement.

"A mentor empowers a person to see a possible future and believe that it can be obtained." ~ **Shawn Hitchcock**

An Uncommon mentor is a picture of your future; the master key to your success in life and they are people who have been where you are going and know the terrain. Their experiences, scars and wisdom will save you from making costly mistakes in life, whether it be in your business, profession, Calling, family, marriage, relationships or in your various leadership roles.

Proverbs 13:20 – *"He who walks with wise men will be wise, but the companion of fools will be destroyed."*

Your Mentors are those who will hold your hand and use their own experiences to teach you so that you do not step on the dangerous landmines they stepped on or make the mistakes they made. It is for you to seek out your Mentors, spend time with them, keep that relationship within appropriate boundaries, and value that relationship.

"A mentor is someone who allows you to see the hope inside yourself."
~ **Oprah Winfrey**

A mentor is a person who can guide you through life, but remember one person cannot mentor you in every aspect of your life (for example your pastor can be your spiritual mentor but not your business mentor).

A mentor is willing to share skills, knowledge and expertise from his own life and experiences.

So, you must seek out mentors who have experience in each of the specific areas of your life (like in business, career, profession, relationships and family etc.) They will see your blind spots which you yourself cannot see and they are able to help you from derailing, deviating or distorting your ordained Purpose and Destiny so as to avoid an abortion of Purpose.

For sound advice and gentle respectful encouragement, commit your loyalty to the right relationships in your life. It's proper you have an older mature Woman, role model to learn from and emulate, one who has been around long enough to know that the hard times do get better and that the coldest winter turns into the most beautiful springs. These mature women provide excellent examples for you as you navigate through the rough terrain in your journey to Destiny.

2 Timothy 1:5 – *"When I call to remembrance the genuine faith that is in you, which dwelt first in your grandmother Lois and your mother Eunice, and I am persuaded is in you also."*

Always remember that as you are being mentored you must also be mentoring others.

"My one criterion for taking on a mentee is that they mentor two other relationships." ~ **Unknown**

Also seek Destiny Coaches are trainers who will help you in different areas of your life (like a general life coach, a business coach, a relationship coach, a style and image coach, a leadership coach or a career coach etc.) They can help you in literally in any area of your life where you need help.

The difference between a mentor and a coach is that a mentor is long term, process based on mutual trust and respect. It is focused on creating an informal association between the mentor and the mentee while a coach is for short term periods of time which follows a more structured and formal approach. A coach supports, guides and trains you in achieving your personal goals, so a coach is solution focused in helping your personal growth and development.

"A coach is someone who tells you what you do not want to hear, who has you see what you don't want to see, so you can be who you have always known you could be." **Tom Landry**

In addition, your Destiny helpers will include positive Role Models, persons whose behaviour, example or success, you can emulate to influence your actions, motivate you to uncover true potentials. They help you to overcome weaknesses, pushes you to strive for higher standards and they act as a testimony that indeed we can.

6. YOUR GATE KEEPERS

These are your sponsors, connectors, investors etc. namely people who give you access to valuable, crucial relationships and resources to enable you fulfil your Calling and Destiny.

"Sponsorship can come to you in different ways, you never know who is watching, so be 'sponsor ready' at all times." ~ **Millette Granville**

Gatekeepers are people who control access to something, somewhere or someone that you need to get to your next level. They control Destiny passwords and are the go between controlling access from one point to another (they can either be positive or negative gate keepers). Your positive gate keepers are Destiny connectors, investors and sponsors.

It is important to have both mentors and sponsors as your Destiny helpers because both play a very key role. While mentors give you perspective, sponsors give you opportunities and while mentors talk with you, sponsors talk about you, while mentors help you skill up, sponsors help you move up.

Gatekeepers of nations are like divine connectors; they have what you are looking for and can help you access that which belongs to you and your generations. They have the influence, ability and connections to bring you to your next level. One introduction from them makes you accepted in circles of greatness.

A word from them makes you receive an appointment letter without any application letters, and they turn your prayer topics into testimonies. In the bible, Joseph was talented but was still in prison, but when he met a gatekeeper of nations in the person of Pharaoh, he became a prime minister within 24 hours.

"You are only one person away from the most important people in the world." ~ **Unknown**

Within months, doors and favours that were impossible to open may just open for you, and without your efforts and you can be automatically connected overnight.

These are persons strategically placed in the echelons of power and authority with powerful networks and associations. They see and recognize your value and potential and are ready to open various doors for you and connect you to what and who you need because they can.

"A friend is one who knows you as you are, understands where you have been, accepts what you have become and still gently allows you to grow." ~ **William Shakespeare**

However, always remember that your sponsor's reputations are on the line regarding how you carry yourself through the doors they open for you, so you must guard these relationships cautiously with utmost respect.

Sponsors are also like referees who vouch for your character and reputation when called upon to do so on the basis that they know you either personally or professionally and can therefore attest to somebody else about you. The quality of their recommendation and reference will depend on their own standing and reputation that gives them the moral authority and mandate to speak for another person.

Your response to having faithful sponsors is to also sponsor other people assigned to you.

"All good leaders are connectors. They relate well and make people feel confident about themselves and their leader." ~**John C. Maxwell.**

Someone once said that the distance between where you are and where you need to be is not kilometers but in heads (for example between you and your healing, prosperity, promotion etc.) This means that the recommendations advice, information, introductions, assistance, favour, mentoring etc. that you need to soar is all about people and relationships.

Connectors are the missing link between who you are and who you were designed to be, but most of the time they look insignificant because they don't have what you are looking for. They look very ordinary but the strange thing about them is that they can connect you to what you are looking for.

In the bible, we find several divine connectors, Naaman was healed of leprosy because there was a maid in his house who became his "divine connector" (2 Kings 5:2). Also, Joseph was the divine connector of the chief cup bearer (Genesis 40:9-14). Saul's servant who recommended David to play the harp for King Saul was David's divine connector (1 Samuel 16:18). Elisha and the Shunamite Woman were each other's divine connector just as Elijah was Elisha's divine connector (2 Kings 4:8). Philip was the divine connector for the Ethiopian eunuch (Acts 8:26-28).

The entrance of divine connectors into your life links you to your future, and an encounter with them causes doors to be opened. Having great potential and gifting with you is not enough without being connected to something or someone you need for your Destiny.

So do not despise people who come into your or who are already in to your life who may not look like they are of any value and relevance to you and your Destiny, but someone around could be your connector to what you need and to your Destiny.

"The point about connectors is that by having a foot in so many different worlds, they have the effect of bringing them all together." ~ **Malcolm Gladwell**

Likewise, you will also be somebody's connector with the same diligence, passion and commitment that your own Destiny connectors have shown you.

Your Destiny connector is one who announces and speaks about your gifts and skills to the right people at strategic places and at the appropriate time. A Destiny connector is an intermediary between you and your Purpose and Destiny.

These Destiny connectors will connect you to people, resources and opportunities that you need in order to get your next level (whether it be in your career, business, ministry, investments, property ownership, leadership etc.)

These connectors, sponsors, investors etc. are your gate keepers, opening the necessary gates to benefit your call and Destiny. However, beware because there can be negative gate keepers who are Destiny killers, who abstract and hinder the gates you need opened. To this extent your positive gate keepers are very important in overcoming, dislodging and overthrowing your negative gate keepers.

7. YOUR DESTINY SPOUSE AND FAMILY

Your spouse is a reflection of your wisdom and a picture of your Destiny. He keeps you focused on your assignments, Calling and Destiny if you have the right spouse. He supports you emotionally, mentally and financially meaning that when you are in the right marriage, your spouse will increase your rate of success. Conversely if you are in a wrong marriage, that spouse will decrease your rate of success and your ability to fulfil your Destiny.

So sadly, but truthfully, your spouse can either be your Destiny helper or your Destiny killer.

Where there is no spouse, then among your family members (whether it be your parents, your siblings, your children, your extended family members as well as your in-laws). There can either be Destiny helpers or Destiny killers.

Parents can shape your Destiny from your very early child hood by instilling the right values and principles, the right emotional and even financial support (where possible) to help you fulfil your Destiny. However, your parents can also hinder your Destiny whether knowingly or unknowingly in their sincere, loving but misguided attempts to help you (especially where they have no revelation as to the who you were born to be and as to what you were created to do). They can push you in the wrong direction away from your Call and Destiny.

Your spouse, parents and family members could also maliciously hinder your Destiny and become Destiny killers where relationships have broken for whatever reasons and there is a lot of toxic bad faith that has crept in between and among you.

Destiny Questions to Ponder On

1. *Have you located your Destiny midwife; what factors enabled you in locating her?*

2. *How did you recognize your burden bearers, what particular characteristics made them stand out?*

3. *What gifts have you found most useful in your gifted Guild?*

4. *What rungs among your ladder holders do you think you are missing?*

5. *How much effort have you put in pursuing your Mentors, Coaches and Role models and what value have they added to you?*

6. *How generous have you gate keepers been, have you ever encountered uncomfortable strings attached to any of your gate keepers, how did you cut those strings?*

7. *In which ways has your spouse and your family being your Destiny helpers or Destiny killers?*

Chapter Four

THE DESTINY KILLERS OF A DESTINY CARRIER

Neutralizing the Forces that Fight Your Destiny

Chapter Preview

94

1. *The Destiny Assassins*

2. *Your Destiny Chokers*

3. *Your Destiny Piercers*

4. *Your Destiny Exploiters*

5. *Your Destiny Saboteurs*

6. *Your Destiny Usurpers*

7. *Your Destiny Emasculators*

OPENING REMARKS

"Demagnetize from Destiny killers, relationships should inspire you not expire you." ~ **Unknown**

Your Destiny will have enemies who will seek to sabotage and kill it. Some will try to kill it before you birth it and others will try to kill it while you are pregnant with it and while you are carrying it and others will try to kill it after you have birthed it.

As women there will be many forces that will seek to oppress, limit derail or delay us from fulfilling our Calling and Destiny, such as cultural traditions and practices that seek to hold women back, discrimination, gender bias and sexual harassment in the work place and in the market place generally, poverty, financial oppression, various forms of abuse, illiteracy etc. Your other Destiny killers include

…your *Destiny Assassins* (your "Herods") and whom you can only defeat through divine wisdom, or

…your *Destiny Chokers,* (your "Harmans") who you can only defeat through powerful intercession and divine strategies,

…your *Destiny Piercers* (your "King Sauls") whom you can only defeat through Righteousness,

…your *Destiny Exploiters* (your "Uncle Labans") who you can only defeat by sharpening and harnessing your skills,

…your *Destiny Saboteurs* (your "Tobias and Sanballats") who you can only defeat by rejecting their hypocrisy and pretentious offers of help,

…your *Destiny Usurpers* (your "Absaloms") who you can only defeat through humility.

…your *Destiny Emasculators* (your "Jezebels") who you can only defeat by casting them out of your lives.

So, in your journey towards Destiny, you will encounter various *Destiny killers* and you must remain alert and guarded and protect your Destiny against all odds. Suffice to say that just as you are endowed and anointed for your Purpose and Destiny you are also endowed and anointed with every weapon you will ever need to out - manoeuvre and overcome every Destiny killer in your path.

The key is to discover those weapons which are within you and around you and to learn how to use them effectively. Your *Destiny killers* will not always come as enemies but disguised as friends and some will even be those who love you dearly but they unknowingly say or do things that can kill your Destiny.

Perhaps your most powerful weapon against your *Destiny killers* is the revelation you have that no one has the power to kill your Destiny but you are the only one who can mess it and prejudice it through sin, disobedience and by willfully neglecting it.

Your *Destiny killers* can only attempt to kill it and they can cause you delays, frustration and prejudice but ultimately, they cannot kill that Destiny (provided that you remain in God's Purpose and will). It is God who ordained that Destiny for you so he will protect it.

Destiny killers steal and obstruct your dreams, they derail your Destiny, they cause delay, they frustrate efforts, they only see the negative side of you, they are kill joys. *Destiny killers* tell you that your Vision is too big, they drag you back, and when they have dreams concerning you, such night dreams are usually of calamity.

These are discouragers, they are wasters (they waste your time and waste your life), they limit you and mock you.

Some *Destiny killers* are in your household, some in your Church, some in your work place etc. and others around you. *Destiny killers* are bent on abolishing your Destiny.

They weaken your faith, and plant seeds of doubt within you by their discouraging and negative comments.

"You need to associate with relationships that inspire you, relationships that challenge yourself to rise higher. Don't waste your valuable time with relationships that are not adding to your growth. Your Destiny is too important." ~ **Joel Osteen**

They plant "tares" among your "wheat" if you dare sleep by losing focus or by not being alert and sensitive to guard your dreams and Visions.

Whether you like it or not you will always have haters in life, the more you do well for yourself the more haters you attract.

Haters hate you because they feel like you are better than them. Haters hate you because they think your life is easier than theirs. Haters hate you because they hate themselves. Haters hate you because they think you don't deserve the life you have. Haters hate you because they have no plans for their lives, but do not worry about what haters, say or do behind your back, focus on your growth and progress. "I have never seen any hater who is doing better than me." **Unknown**

In short, these enemies of your Destiny also include your adversary, who is your opponent, your rival, combatant and Contender, who seek to out-maneuver you in your efforts. He is your enemy and the enemy of your Destiny.

1.   THE DESTINY ASSASSINS

Assassination is the eliminating of a public figure especially who holds immense power and authority. A time will come when the impact and influence that your Calling is making causes you to become known, recognized, celebrated and feared by your enemies who will then try to "eliminate" you by derailing your call and Destiny so as to kill it.

So, a Destiny *assassin* is an enemy who knows that your Purpose is a threat to him. He knows that the impact of your Purpose will hinder and eliminate what he stands for and your Purpose threatens his very existence.

They know that you and your Purpose will overthrow them and their wicked plans. They will seek to trick those who are celebrating your, and plot and scheme how to access you and kill you. Sometimes your Destiny assassinators will seek to eliminate you and your Purpose at the point when you are birthing it because even at that early stage, they know about your great potential that will unleash and displace them.

When they do not know how to access you and your Calling, they use those to whom it has been revealed. Hence the reason you must guard against those to whom you reveal your dreams and visions (especially at the early stage, when it is vulnerable and easy to kill).

Your Destiny assassins will never do the dirty job themselves; they prefer to hide behind the scenes and hire "Destiny hit men" who they have groomed to do it for them. Their aim is to stop you from becoming who you were born to be or to stop you from continuing to do what you were created for. This is the "Herod spirit" (Mathew 2:16)

The characteristics of a Destiny assassin are extreme insecurity, paranoia, manipulation, delusional, cunningness, powers of persuasion, betrayal etc. the assassination plot targets your character and reputation. They use exaggeration and manipulation to spread malicious false reports and accusations, slander, libel, and defamation so as to discredit your integrity, morality etc. in the eyes of people who matter to you. The ultimate intention is to dilute your authority and influence.

"Attempts at character assassination occur when it is too conspicuous to pierce your target with a bullet." **Sardonyx Jade**

Sometimes the assassination is motivated by need for revenge (an avenging complex where they perceive you have wronged them or even jealousy where you appear to be outshining them).

Your Destiny assassins are never strangers but usually people around you with whom you are serving or working together who know you well enough and have a revelation of the greatness within you. They know you are the "real deal" and they fear that you are better than them and that you will dislodge them from their positions.

Assassination also includes destroying your support systems and structures as a way of weakening you power and effectiveness. They are threatened by your power and prominence, especially where they fear that your Calling entails confronting and eliminating their wickedness (like corruption, sexual perversity, witchcraft, idolatry, oppression and dictatorship etc.)

Your weapon against Destiny assassins is divine wisdom to hide your visions, dreams, plans and strategies. Guard and sieve who you surround yourself.

2. YOUR DESTINY CHOKERS

This enemy seeks to hinder you from fulfilling your Purpose once you have discovered it and once you have decided to fulfil it by "hanging it on gallows". They are usually positioned in your place of assignment, seeking to outshine and outdo everyone else. Taking and claiming credit, accolades and public celebration for other people's good work and labour.

This is the "Harman spirit" that seeks your down fall. *(Esther 5:14)*

They are usually close to the source of power so they have the opportunity to access those in power by lying and giving them false information and false accusations about you and others. They seek to discredit you in the eyes your leaders and authorities. So, it is important that you remain humble and submitted to your leaders and authorities because ultimately, they will see the truth.

So, in short, this Destiny choker obstructs your Purpose and Destiny;

- Falsely accusing you so as to make you to lose favour and your position of influence whether in the family, church, society, organization, Government etc. or wherever you are positioned.
- By despising and being very critical of your beliefs and values and operating with a persecution agenda against you and your people leaning towards a genocidal tendency.
- Misinterpreting your motives and agendas and portraying them as sinister and evil.
- Seeking to destroy you and remove you from your position of favour so that they take it for themselves and reap rewards and harvests they do not deserve.

You must therefore outsmart this enemy by having a powerful intercessory plan and strategic exploits. You must draw on your networks to assist you (using wisdom to get favour) and submitting to the advice and counsel of your mentors and Destiny mid-wives so that you can get access to your leaders and disclose the wicked schemes of these enemies. In the Bible Harman was Esther's Destiny Choker.

As an Esther you understand that through wise strategy you can get favour from the king. He will extend his sceptre to you signifying his acceptance and favour which reveals and reinforces who you were in that place, your self-identity, your Purpose and your power in that place. Meaning, that ultimately at your place of Purpose you are more powerful than your Destiny chokers.

Your response to these *Destiny chokers* and obstructers is to focus on your assignment and Purpose knowing that they have no power to hinder you, if you use the right strategy in godly wisdom.

Consequently, your aim is not to attack or waste time confronting these chokers and the obstructers but instead to let them think they have gotten victory over you. While they are in their false sense of security, you put a strategy into place and outsmart them as you ride on to your Destiny.

Your revelation as to why you are in powerful and privileged positions whether in church, Government, market place etc. is perhaps your most powerful weapon against these Destiny chokers because that revelation empowers you to arise and in authority defeat them as you fulfil your Purpose there.

The one good thing about Destiny chokers and obstructers is that they force you out of your comfort zone and provoke you to push and stretch yourself and fulfil your Purpose and Destiny.

The gallows these *Destiny chokers* had built for you, eventually become their own gallows upon which they hang miserably. You must be ready to take great risks, and possibly great suffering to silence this enemy and fulfil your Purpose.

3. YOUR DESTINY PIERCERS

This piercer has a spear to pin you and your Destiny against the wall and silence you. The spear here symbolizes a weapon of authority and power. This enemy is usually in a position of leadership and power in your place of assignment, but by virtue of their failure to follow required steps in fulfilling their Purpose, they disqualify themselves and you become their substitute to take over, from them.

Your *Destiny piercer* knows that you are his replacement to fulfil the Purpose he failed to fulfil, so he sees you as a great threat and therefore tries to spear and kill you and your Purpose and Destiny. This piercer is vexatious hounds you day and night, stalks you with intimidation, threats, guilt and force accusation. This is the "spear of Saul" spirit. (1 Samuel 19)

This Destiny piercer could be in your family, church, business, place of work, political leadership arena or whatever organization and institution where you may be operating.

While it is clear you are replacing a Destiny piercer, their tenure has not actually expired and pending that expiry, you are under a test to see your ability to survive such adverse circumstances and attacks without taking matters into your own hands by revenging.

"If you don't take an opponent serious, they surprise you." ~ **Canelo Alvarez**

The motives and intentions of your Destiny Piercer and adversary is to destroy you and your Destiny, render you totally ineffective, attack and criticise your every effort, engage in dubious clandestine methods of derailing you and your Destiny.

Your strategy is to handle these enemies very carefully. There is usually a paradoxical relationship between you, and them because they are either your leaders or bosses under whom you're still positioned.

The fact that your *Destiny piercer* is a leader and authority in your life (whether in the family, market place, Government, church etc.) who is still in power and so you must respect and honour, him makes this Destiny killer very difficult to deal with.

The best way to respond and relate to your Destiny Piercer is to remain alert and sensitive, guarded against his schemes and strategies, and continue focusing on fulfilling your Purpose and Destiny undeterred.

Your most powerful weapons against this enemy are;

- By using Wisdom and swiftness in escaping the spear
- By honouring and respecting the office of this piercer because he is still an authority.
- By keeping your distance.
- By connecting to your allies who will help you by disclosing to you the strategies of this piercer so you can escape.

Beware of wasting your precious energy and time by devising wicked and evil, schemes and strategies against your adversary. Cunningness will lower and demean you to their despicable level and make you no better than them. Let this enemy know that if you wanted to, you would easily destroy him, but you choose not to avenge yourself, and to trust in God and God's timing.

In outsmarting your *Destiny Piercer*, you must ensure to retain and maintain your dignity and decorum, and your focus on your Purpose and Destiny, walking righteously and you will grow stronger and stronger as this enemy grows weaker and weaker.

"Move fast. Speed is one of your main advantages over large competitors." ~ **Sam Altman**

4. YOUR DESTINY EXPLOITERS

To exploit is to treat someone unfairly in order to benefit from their hard work and labour but it can also extend to sexual and emotional exploitation etc. This is an enemy that also seeks to hinder you from fulfilling your Purpose by oppressing, enslaving, tormenting and exploiting you and keeping you stagnant and bound in fruitless labour for his own benefit, by also hindering you from going to your place of Purpose. This is the "uncle Laban spirit" (Genesis 29)

These are usually employers or other leaders you may be serving in whichever sphere whether in the family, church, work place, business enterprise, government etc.

Another dimension of this Destiny exploiter is to keep short-changing you by constantly changing the goal posts and rules. So, you slog and labour for him without a right reward. You must eventually escape and go fulfil your Purpose.

These enemies are like freeloaders who are users, parasites, leeches, spongers, hangers-on, and free riders who take much more than they give, who want to be supported by others without adequate return to support others.

This is the kind of person who is lazy, lethargic and seeks to derail you and defocus you from your own assignments and responsibilities to you own detriment and seriously prejudicing your Destiny. This enemy seeks to use you to accomplish their own goals but never helps you to accomplish yours.

"Thought, like any parasite cannot exist without a compliant host."
~ **Bernard Beckett**

Your strategy against these enemies is to remain persistent and resilient despite every frustration until you become a stench to their nostrils and they let you go. After having exploited you and bound you for so long, this enemy must suffer the consequences by releasing to you what is rightfully yours, because you will need it for fulfilling your Purpose and Destiny.

The way to relate and respond to a freeloader is to master the power of saying NO. You must resist every deception that derails you and compromises your Destiny. You must resist any one who seeks to deplete and divert your resources, time and energy for the wrong Purposes. A freeloader is like a parasite or a tick that sucks the energy out of a hardworking person, leaving you drained and empty.

"Light attracts light. But sometimes your light attracts moths and your warmth attracts parasites. Protect your space and energy."
~**Warsan Shire**

The important thing to remember is that in your journey to Destiny you are not assigned to everybody. You are not supposed to engage, interact or help everyone in the world and likewise not everyone is assigned to be your portion or helper.

In fact, some who may purport to help you in fulfilling your Calling will be more instrumental in killing it than helping it. So, learn to pray and discern who your real Destiny helpers are and more importantly to repel those who are not assigned as your Destiny helpers.

Your best weapons against your Destiny exploiters are;

- To acquire new skills and to harness and sharpen the skills you already have. Enhance your self-growth and development and be able to be productive and fruitful without having to be enslaved by another.
- Learn how to negotiate effectively for what you deserve and that which is proportionate to your hard work and labour.
- Exchange your cunning and deceptive traits for pure and honest work ethics.
- Learn to strategize smartly and wisely so that you may plan your exit from the oppression of your Destiny exploiter.

5. YOUR DESTINY SABOTEURS

"Make sure everybody in your boat is rowing and not drilling holes when you are not looking. Know your circle." **Unknown**

Sabotage is deliberate underhanded action to interfere, derail, destroy and subvert another person's effort, property and welfare out of envy, jealousy and malice etc.

This enemy is a *Destiny saboteur*, pretending to be supportive of your Purpose but secretly seeking to sabotage it, so be careful who you allow to assist you in your Purpose but guard against those who are not your designated Destiny helpers and connectors.

A *Destiny saboteur* who is basically one who is jealous and envious of your position, zeal and passion, resents the progress and milestones you are achieving and therefore seeks to derail you by carrying out hidden and sinister counteractions that hinder and undermine your progress. Often unknown to you. It is usually the people around you who have access to information etc. about you.

Another wicked device this enemy may use is to plant seeds of doubt, fear, discouragement while pretending to express concern and offer wise counsel. Beware of those who express undue interest in you and your Purpose and who offer unsolicited advice and assistance. They will sabotage your valuable relationships, opportunities, success etc.

Your strategy against this enemy is to reject their help and assistance and disconnect any ties you may have with them. The best way to respond and relate to your saboteurs is to walk in extreme wisdom and discernment always a step ahead of them and without allowing them to know that you know their schemes against you and resisting their assistance and hiding your plans.

Remember your saboteurs are discouragers who often try to tell you that your Vision is too large for you to bear etc. wickedly seeking to mislead you to give up and quit, and thereby abandon your Destiny. So, flee from your Destiny saboteurs. (Nehemiah 4) This is the "Tobias or Sanballat" spirit

"Some people aren't satisfied until they sabotage someone else's happiness. Be careful who you trust, not everyone who smiles at you is a friend." **Unknown**

6.   YOUR DESTINY USURPERS

Other enemies of your Destiny are those who seek to usurp it and take it for themselves by hijacking it and forcefully claiming your Visions and projects as their own. They illegally supplant themselves in your family, church, business, organization or church. Destiny Usurpers are those who have either not discovered their own Purposes or have aborted them so they are seeking to steal yours.

A usurper seizes what is yours forcefully and illegally, but that wrongful grabbing of power does not give him legitimate authority over you what is yours. He or she cannot get far. A Destiny usurper makes himself more important than he is to appear powerful by putting himself in a position of importance.

He endears himself to your followers, pretending to care for them more than you do, by giving them false attention and force humility. That way, he places himself between you and your relationships and he begins to question your authority and wisdom so as to weaken your influence in the eyes of those you are leading.

This is the "Absalom spirit" (2 Samuel 15)

He plays on their human fear giving them the impression that they need him and without him they are doomed.

A Destiny usurper seeks to take over your vision, Calling, relationships, resources and everything you had available to fulfil your Purpose. He purports to be the one more suited to fulfil that Purpose. The most painful thing is that often your usurper is normally from among your inner circle (either some of your supporters or a protégé etc.) who already have insider knowledge about you and your Purpose, which they use to betray and undermine you, by inciting your most loyal supporters to lure them away.

Sometimes these usurpers of your Destiny are vicious enemies who are under you, serving you and allegedly supporting your Vision but greed for power makes them over throw you so that they become the leader and owner of that Vision.

The way to handle Destiny usurper is to expose them and to reveal their evil motives to your Destiny Helpers so that their credibility can be questioned and you can safeguard and protect your relationships. The aim of a Destiny usurper is to execute you and all other possible claimants, successors and inheritors of your Vision.

7. YOUR DESTINY EMASCULATORS

This enemy seeks to suffocate and stifle you and your Purpose by disempowering you and making you limp and voiceless and completely unable to fulfil your Purpose. A Destiny emasculator intimidates, manipulates and harasses you into silence and inactivity, whereby you lose all strength, confidence and esteem. You become a powerless tool in their wicked hands so they can misuse you, and derail you from your Purpose and Destiny.

Emasculators deprive you of your self-identity and true roles making you weak and crippled emotionally and mentally, and kill your spirit, zeal and passion for your Purpose and Destiny.

The intention of your Destiny emasculator is to make you a eunuch, powerless and impotent unable to fulfil your Purpose and Destiny.

You must therefore remain alert and sensitive guard against all these Destiny killers who are quite subtle in their approach and who often come as angels of light to catch you unawares.

One way of remaining protected from the adverse effects of Destiny killers is by clinging to your Destiny helpers thereby leaving no room or door for Destiny killers to access your life.

"A Eunuch is a man who has had his work cut out for him." ~ **Robert Burns**

The wicked emasculator of your Destiny is a "Jezebel spirit" (1 Kings 21) because Jezebel makes you co-dependent on her for strength and so when you draw your strength. She seeks to control you and use you to serve her evil Purposes.

Your most powerful weapon against this Destiny emasculator is to be very strong in handling the sword meaning the word of God in your mouth.

Destiny Questions to Ponder On

1. *Have you ever encountered a Destiny assassinator; how did you escape the assassin's bullet?*

2. *Have you ever been chocked by a Destiny chocker, how did you disentangle yourself from his grasp?*

3. *Have you ever been pinned by a Destiny Piercer; how did you escape?*

4. *Have you ever encountered a Destiny exploiter, what strategies did you use to outmanoeuvre her?*

5. *What in your opinion is the most effective shield against internal or external Destiny saboteurs?*

6. *What are the subtle tactics of a Destiny usurper that may catch you unaware?*

7. *How do you recognize a Destiny emasculator and how do you distance yourself from such?*

Chapter Five

THE SIBLING RIVALS IN A DESTINY FAMILY

Diffusing Family Conflicts That Threaten Your Destiny

Chapter Preview

1. **A Competitive Sisterhood**

   (*Sister barren beauty vs sister fertile squing eyes*)

2. **A Fattened Calf Affair**

   (*Sister perfect vs sister prodigal*)

3. **A Legitimacy Legend**

   (*Sister chosen vs sister sideline*)

4. **A Birth right Battle**

   (*Sister zeal vs sister apathy*)

5. **A Fatal Envy**

   (*Sister diligent vs sister negligent*)

6. **A Colourful Coat Contention**

   (*Sister dream chaser vs sister dream killer*)

7. **A Leprosy Penalty**

   (*Sister destiny climber vs side ladder holder*)

OPENING REMARKS

"You are born into your family and your family is born into you. No returns. No exchanges." ~ Elizabeth Berg

In the process of fulfilling your Purpose and going to your Destiny there are several members of your biological family that may play a key role in ushering you to your Destiny, and others who will act as hindrances and obstacles.

Unlike other relationships where you choose who you will relate with and to what extent and even decide when to disconnect and "drop" such relationships, your family members are not optional choices, so you must learn how to manage these delicate family relationships so as not to jeopardize your Purpose and Destiny.

"You don't choose your family; they are God's gift to you as you are to them." ~ Desmond Tutu

Regarding your siblings, there will be a myriad of subtle enmities, contentions, conflicts, envies, competitive spirits, animosities, birth right battles, legitimacy claims, colourful coat contentions etc. arising from various factors and some leading to regrettable consequences.

"Family is conflict and it's something we all relate to." ~ Bill Cosby

Your "FAMILY" in this context firstly refers to your biological family whether nuclear, extended or in-laws, and it also includes your home "church family", your "business family", your "work place family", "social network family", and any other such groupings where you have become close enough to consider yourselves a "Family".

"It's not blood that makes a family, its love." ~ Unknown

1. A COMPETITIVE SISTERHOOD

(Sister Barren Beauty Vs Sister Fertile Squint Eyes)

**"Sibling Rivalry sometimes leads to the bitterest competitions."
Unknown**

In every kind of family, for every **"Sister Barren Beauty Queen"**, there is a **"Sister Fertile Squinty Eyes"**.

A woman will have competition in whatever kind of family she is in, which will have an impact on her life and Destiny. For example, when they see that she is the one who is favoured, preferred and at an advantage. When she is perceived as the outwardly attractive and presentable Woman and the one who everyone wants. Whereas her competitor may be one whose outward packaging is not so attractive nor presentable.

The irony, however is that she maybe the Woman who is outwardly attractive is the barren and unproductive, and whereas though outwardly unattractive her competitor may be the one who is fruitful and productive.

"Sister is probably the most competitive relationships within the family, but once the sisters are grown, it becomes the strongest relationship." ~ Margaret Mead

This means that we must never judge a book by its cover because a divine reversal may take place and her competitor may get the advantage over her. We cannot prejudge the worth or value of something or someone by its outward cover.

Sometimes in whatever type of "family" you are in, you will find yourself highly favoured because of your outward appearance like beauty, the way you present yourself thereby giving the impression that you are fruitful and productive. However, in reality you are not and this fact only becomes evident after you have been chosen over others around you whose physical appearance and presentation gives the impression that they are not fruitful and productive.

When we are dealing with a competitive sisterhood there are several factors as follows;

- One sister is outwardly attractive is nonetheless inwardly barren unproductive and unfruitful. This means that she may have the good outward qualities of charisma articulation in speech as being well spoken, presentable and sociable etc. but inwardly she is dry, barren, unfruitful and unproductive in the sense that she cannot bring forth fruit (in terms of success in her relationships, work place, business etc.) So, she is chosen and preferred purely for her outward good qualities.
- The other sister is inwardly fertile, fruitful and productive, able to bring forth fruit (in terms of success in the work place, fruit relationships, in her business) but outwardly she is not attractive or presentable so she is chosen purely because of her inward fertility.
- The outwardly attractive (but inwardly barren) sister will be envious of the other sister who is inwardly fertile. While the inwardly fertile sister will be envious of the outwardly attractive sister. In other words, each sister wants what the other sister has and hence the competition. They try to outdo each other where each one uses their strength to mock the other's weaknesses.
- What the barren sister doesn't realize is that she does not need to compete with her fertile sister nor does she need to incite people to reject her fertile sister on the grounds that she is not attractive. Instead, this barren sister should focus on seeking how to break her barrenness. She must realize that her barrenness has not been caused by her sister's fertility nor can that barrenness be broken by her fertile sister losing her fertility.

- On the other hand, what the fertile sister does not realize is that she does not need to compete with her attractive sister, nor does she need to incite people to reject her beautiful sister because of her barrenness. Instead, this fertile sister should focus on accepting and seeing herself as beautiful, fearfully and wonderfully made (despite people's opinions) and she must realize that her lack of outward attractiveness in the eyes of others has not been caused by her sister's outward attractiveness nor can her lack of attractiveness in the eyes of others be changed by her sister losing her beauty.

- The epicentre of this kind of envy and competition is usually one man or a group of persons in the family that have made these two women insecure. It causes a lot of hurt to the innocent people around these two sisters and it also derails them and distracts them from focusing on their Callings and Destiny. It erodes their self-identity so seriously because they are seeking to define themselves with the wrong things which only leads to an identity crisis.

- If you are the outwardly attractive but inwardly barren sister, in this scenario then the solution is for you to stop envying your fertile sister. Seek how you can also be fertile, productive and fruitful and what you need to do in order to become sufficient in the areas that you are deficient.
  Where your barrenness is in respect of a physical baby then you must be careful to guard against allowing yourself to defined by your ability or inability to bear children, because there is so much more value in you beyond bearing physical children.

- And where your barrenness is in your finances, business, work place or in your social relational life, then all you need to do is discover and unleash your hidden potential. Let the gifts and the talents within you manifest. Acquire the necessary skills etc. in order to break the barrenness in those areas. Learn how to create wealth, become productive in your vocation and how to develop and maintain meaningful relationships etc. More importantly know that your value and relevance should come from your ability to discover and fulfil your Calling and Destiny.

- And if you are the fertile sister who is outwardly unattractive (in the eyes of others) then you must also refuse to be defined by other people's opinions (on what is attractive). You must also refuse to be defined by your ability to bear physical children, because with or without children you are valuable as an individual. Your relevance and value should not come because of having children but rather by your ability to discover and fulfil your Calling and Destiny.

- If you are the beautiful yet barren sister, the best way for you to respond to this kind of rivalry is to use the provocation from your fertile sister positively and focus on breaking your barrenness (instead of focusing on becoming bitter and distracted by your sister's fertility and fruitfulness).

- Also remember that your barrenness will be broken when you stop focusing on the non-essentials like outward beauty and instead you focus on the things that matter and that pertain to your Calling and Destiny. Your outward beauty and attractiveness no matter how much you may be chosen and preferred because of it, will not and cannot break your barrenness.

- And if you are the fertile sister (yet outwardly unattractive), then your right response is to refuse the rejection and negative labelling and instead to gracefully let your fruitfulness manifest itself and prove your rejecters wrong.

Do not taunt or mock your barren beauty queen sister and do not become bitter towards those who rejected you. Just remember that you are not defined by other people's opinions and your true self-identity is to be found in the one who made you fertile and fruitful. Do not allow your insecurities (because of your outward appearance) to overshadow the beauty of your fertility, fruitfulness and productivity.

"Love is close to hate when it comes to sisters. You're as close as two humans can be. You came from the same womb. The same background, even if you're poles apart, mentally. That's why it hurts so much when your sister is unkind. It's as though part of you is turning against yourself." ~ Jane Corry

2. A FATTENED CALF AFFAIR

(*Sister perfect vs sister prodigal*)

**"Entitlement is a delusion built on self-centeredness and laziness."
Unknown**

In every kind of family for every **Sister Perfect** there will be a **Sister Prodigal.** This is where you are either the very selfish and irresponsible sister and you seriously mess up often, but when you return and retrace your steps and are forgiven your perfect responsible sister is offended because she prefers to have you written- off for your mistakes and judged eternally.

Do you often find yourself as the **"sister prodigal"** constantly messing and disappointing those who are trying to nurture you for Destiny. When you become impatient and seek to do things in your own way without any wise counsel and mentorship. When you disconnect from your Destiny helpers, only to hit a dead end and come crawling back to your family (whether it be a church family, business family, social family). Do they always forgive, forbear, and redeem you with second chances.

"What separates privileges from entitlement is gratitude." ~ **Brene Brown**

Or are you the **"sister perfect"** who is very obedient, faithful and trustworthy in whichever family you are in but somehow the focus and attention is always on the prodigal sister who is always given chance after chance.

A "**sister perfect**" you are the responsible Woman who does things right and you feel unappreciated and taken advantage of for your good behaviour and responsibility and you resent and condemn your sibling when she is forgiven and redeemed.

"Any fool can criticize, complain, and condemn—and most fools do. But it takes character and self-control to be understanding and forgiving." Dale Carnegie

As a "**sister perfect**", the responsible self-righteous sister you must learn to forbear and accommodate the mistakes and weaknesses of others and extend forgiveness and grace.

And as "**sister Prodigal**" the irresponsible sister you must not take advantage of the forgiveness and grace extended to you again and again as a sign to repeat or continue in your prodigal patterns of behaviour.

The other response to this sibling rivalry if you are "**Sister Perfect**", is to focus on fulfilling your own Purpose and Destiny and remain expectant for your own rewards without getting distracted by your "**Sister Prodigal**" when she messes.

Do not begrudge her when she is given a second chance, because your Calling and Purpose is different from hers and so are your rewards. The fact that she is redeemed every time she messes, does not decrease your rewards and it does not affect your Purpose and Destiny in any way.

As "**Sister Perfect**" be grateful for your strengths and self-discipline and be sensitive and accommodate the weaknesses and struggles in others. Never be too confident in self-regarding your strengths and abilities because it is by grace that you have been able to walk right.

The reservoir from where the forgiveness, forbearance, grace and favour (that your "**sister prodigal**" gets whenever she messes) will not dry up and it does not mean that the more she gets that forgiveness, forbearance, grace and favour, the reservoir will have none left over for you. In other words, her being forgiven does not deny you anything or take anything away from you.

The fact that your "**sister prodigal**" gets a fattened calf slaughtered a clean cloak and a ring, does not mean that there is none left over for you. Your own fattened calf, cloak and ring will always be there (meaning that your blessings do not get reduced just because another person gets blessed). Your hardness of heart is blinding and hindering you from seeing that, and your self-righteousness is coming from a cold hard place from within you that you must address and deal with. Today your "**sister prodigal**" will be the one down and messy but tomorrow it could be you. Remember that your parents and leaders in whatever family it may be etc. have a responsibility to love and restore the weak. They are anointed and equipped for it, so do not judge or criticize them for doing what they have been assigned to do. In fact, it is the goodness and mercy that we extend to others that actually changes them and reforms them. You should be patient and allow your "**sister prodigal**" to get as many chances as possible so that hopefully and eventually she will be reformed.

As "**sister perfect**" do not allow the bitterness in your heart to derail you on focusing from your Call and Destiny.

"Teach your children gratefulness. Do all you can to deliver them from our culture's poisonous entitlement mentality." ~ **Randy Alcorn**

3. A LEGITIMACY LEGEND

(*Sister chosen vs sister sideline*)

"Never stop doing your best just because someone doesn't give you credit." ~ Unknown

Matthew 22:14 "For many are called, but few are chosen."

In every kind of family, for every **Sister Chosen** there will be a **Sister Side-lined**.

Maybe you are the chosen one, favoured and preferred but you are taking too long to manifest, and to unleash your potential and become the who you were born to be and do what you were created to do (not because of any fault of your own. Sometimes the Destiny within you is so great, that it takes longer for you to be made and moulded so that you can fulfil it. Those awaiting for your manifestation become impatient of waiting and they seek alternatives.

In fact, "**sister chosen**" will not usually look the part and although the family knows she is the chosen and preferred one, they may begin to doubt it because of the absence of anything in her to testify to that greatness.

The absence of any extraordinarily achievements, leads the family to sincerely assume that perhaps there was nothing special about her after all. This is simply because the real her has not yet manifested.

So, in a family (whether it be a biological family, business family, church, or a work place family or even a social group family) someone may be chosen for certain roles, positions, privileges, mandates, benefits or even leadership and succession by the authorities within that family, yet that person who has been chosen does not reflect or live up to the expectations of those who have chosen her.

On the other hand, there may be another sister who is clearly manifesting and living up to the tasks, assignments and responsibilities that have been marked out for the chosen sister. The authorities in that family are quite happy in her doing so and in fact they continue to assign her these roles and responsibilities. However, this performing sister continues to be side-lined and taken for granted and not recognized nor is she officially given the position of the chosen sister.

The reason that the authorities in such a family assign this role to **sister side-lined** is because they have become impatient in waiting for **sister chosen** to manifest and mature to that position. So, they prefer to take shortcuts and to use **sister side-lined** who is available and ready but unfortunately **sister side-lined** becomes collateral damage when **sister chosen** finally manifests and comes to take up her rightful position. This may lead to a vicious sibling rivalry.

Sister chosen is the original real deal, whereas **sister side-lined** is the alternative who is used, while awaiting for the **chosen sister.**

This is where we must remember that favour is not fair and often, we may not agree with or understand the reasons why one is chosen and another one is not chosen.

Sometimes parents or leaders may make the mistake of favoring and preferring some of their children or followers to take up certain seats and positions which were not ordained for those children or followers that they have selected in the flesh without seeking God's mind. This often has unfortunate consequences whereby God ultimately installs those He had actually ordained for those seats and positions leaving the ones who had been chosen in the flesh to suffer the rejection and confusion. In addition, this kind of carnal favoritism may seriously prejudice and jeopardize the Destinies of such children and followers.

"**Sister side-lined**" will delight at the delayed manifestation of **sister chosen**, hoping that sister chosen never manifests, and when she does manifest sister side-lined will mock, taunt and intimidate her in order to silence her from becoming the 'who' she was born to be and from doing what she was created to do.

What **sister side-lined** must remember is that even though she might have taken up the role and position of **sister chosen** for a while and even though she may have performed to some level of satisfaction, nonetheless as long as **sister chosen** is available and willing, then she (sister side-lined) could never legitimately fulfil that role and position the way the one chosen for it can.

"An Ishmael will always mock an Isaac." ~ Unknown

If you find yourself in this sibling rivalry and you find yourself as the **sister chosen** then your response is to ignore the intimidations of **sister side-lined** and accept your rightful position as the chosen one and proceed to manifest and meet the expectations of those who have been waiting for you.

And if you find yourself as the **sister side-lined** then remember that it was not your fault that you found yourself having to play the role and position of **sister chosen**. It is the fault of those who placed you there in their own misguided notion that that's where you belonged or used you there as they waited for sister chosen.

So, when **sister chosen** arrives to take up her rightful place from you, do not strive for that which was never yours. With much grace, dignity and wisdom, move on and seek to discover your rightful place and position where you will be the **Sister Chosen** and not the **Sister Side-lined** and where you will be rightfully celebrated and not just tolerated.

There is a place for each and every one of us. We are each special and uniquely gifted and endowed to become who we were born to be and not become someone else. We must do what we were created to do and not what another person was created to do.

In many nations of the world, it is not surprising to find that the heads of state, kings and queens are people who the families did not expect. Even though deep down they may have known that these were the chosen ones who they decided to ignore. Yet ultimately the chosen ones rose to the occasion.

So, to avoid this kind of sibling rivalry if you are **sister chosen**, take up your rightful place boldly without fear and fulfil your call and Destiny without allowing any intimidation to deter you. If you are **sister side-lined**, you must accept the inevitable and let go of any positions and Callings that are not rightfully yours. Be ready to discover your own Calling in your right place and sphere where you will fulfil it with your head held high.

4. A BIRTH RIGHT BATTLE

(*Sister zeal vs sister apathy*)

In every family, for every "**Sister Zeal**" there will be "**Sister Apathy**".

This is where there is an assumption that **sister apathy** is the automatic choice and candidate for whatever position privileges etc. that the family has. Yet "**Sister Zeal**" is so alert and passionate for Purpose and Destiny that she somehow manages to outdo "**Sister Apathy**" in every situation and get ahead. She may even use sister apathy's weaknesses to snatch that which allegedly "belongs" to "**sister apathy**" for herself.

Perhaps what nobody understands is that "**Sister Zeal**" is actually the one who was the real entitled and who has what it takes. So that, her taking what everyone thought was **sister's apathy's** is actually just taking what truly belong to her.

A **Sister zeal** somehow understands and has some revelation about the things that matter and the power of a birth right and hence the reason she "persuades" Sister apathy into giving it up. Whereas **sister apathy** is one with no revelation about the things that matter nor about the power of her birth right so she operates in the flesh and chooses that which is carnal and worldly with instant gratification and forfeits that which is divine and eternal.

If you are **sister zeal** within a family (whatever type it may). You may find that you are really the one entitled for a particular position, privilege and mandate etc. Yet somebody else (whether because they are older chronologically by age or more educated or of male gender) is assumed to be the one or where there is a succession plan or mantles to be inherited and it is erroneously assumed that the successor or the inheritor is **sister apathy**. Yet in reality it is you, then you must be ready to claim and lay hold of that which is yours legitimately.

As a typical sister zeal, you may seek to take advantage of your sister apathy's weaknesses and trick her by negotiating and offering her something you know she is interested in (usually something temporal and carnal) in exchange for that which she is holding (which is often priceless and eternal but which she doesn't even value anyway). She may be quite ready to surrender it to you in exchange for what you are offering her. Sister apathy may much later on realize that you have tricked her and she will seek to revenge.

As a **Sister Zeal**, you must beware of the anger and wrath from your **Sister Apathy** (for your actions against her) but more importantly you must lay hold of that which is now yours and run with it, and keep yourself separated and hidden from your Sister Apathy's wrath and anger until the right time.

As entitled as you are (as **sister zeal**) it is important to acknowledge that your deceptive methods of obtaining what was yours from **sister apathy** means that you need a "character overhaul". This is a painful process that you must undergo to mould your character, mature you and enable you to let go of deceptive methods and adopt the right methods so that you may lay a strong righteous foundation as you embark to fulfil your Destiny.

You must however always remember that your **sister apathy** is a nightmare waiting to revenge. You will need to grow in wisdom and strategy in order to diffuse your **sister apathy's** wrath and revenge. Fortunately, having undergone the radical process of your character overhaul, you will be able to appease your **sister apathy** when the time comes, so that you may both agree to peacefully pursue your own Callings and Destiny.

So, in this kind of scenario a time will come when you will need to stop hiding from your angry sibling. You must get ready to confront your fear of her, otherwise that fear may stand in the way of your Destiny. You may surprisingly find that over the years the anger and desire for revenge has ended and your **sister apathy** has long discovered her place in life and is already fulfilling her own Calling and Destiny and she is not interested in yours.

5. A FATAL ENVY

(Sister diligent vs sister negligent)

"Envy is a fatal poison which spoils souls." ~ Benjamin Jonson

In a family for every **Sister Diligent** there will be a **Sister Negligent**.

Sometimes in a family, business, church, organization or any other sector etc. there are those who are more diligent intentional and Purposeful in what is expected of them. They are more committed and dedicated and very focused, passionate and serious about their Calling and Destiny than the others.

Sister Diligent is one who has revelation on what is important and right to those having authority over her etc. She is diligent and sensitive to listen and hear the right voices and feel the heartbeat of those that matter and those above her. She is therefore able to discern what they require of her, so that she diligently aligns herself because she knows it will impact her Purpose and Destiny positively.

She is therefore a Destiny chaser. Whereas **sister negligent** is not alert and sensitive to the voices or heartbeat of those that matter and those above her. She relies more on her own strength and understanding and thereby ends up performing below that which is expected of her and that which is necessary for her Calling and Destiny.

If you are **sister diligent**, then your **sister negligent** will begrudge and hate you for doing right and will take out her frustrations of failure on you, and even seek to blame you for her setbacks and for her failure to fulfil her Calling and Destiny.

So, your **sister negligent** in her misdirected rage seeks to destroy and kill you and your Destiny. So, you must separate yourself from her wisely so that you may safely fulfil your own Calling and Destiny. This is perhaps the most dangerous sibling rivalry because in some cases, your **sister's negligent** rage may turn murderous and uncontrollable.

Many **sister diligent** types whether they are leaders, business persons, church leaders, corporate heads etc. have been killed physically, emotionally or spiritually in this kind of scenario and their ability to fulfil their Purpose and Destiny silenced forever. So, if you find yourself in a family surrounded by a **sister negligent**, you must take every measure to protect your life, Purpose and Destiny from this murderous rage and spirit.

If you are a **sister negligent** in this scenario, then you must stop your misguided notion that your failures are caused by your **sister diligent** and instead stop and seek advice from your **sister diligent** and ask her what she is doing in order to be successful, allow her to teach you and guide you instead of blaming her.

In addition, it is important you find out from your **sister diligent** what is this Destiny that she keeps chasing, what is it about and how can you know about it, how you can discover your Calling and embark on fulfilling it. You should also ask your **sister diligent** how you can hear the right voices and how you can align yourself to what is expected of you so that you may do right by those who are above you and also get your rewards.

6. A COLOURFUL COAT CONTENTION

(Sister dream chaser vs sister dream killer)

Proverbs 28:21 *"To show partiality is not good, because for a piece of bread a man will transgress."*

In any family, for every **Sister Dream Chaser** there will be a **Sister Dream killer.**

This is where you find you are a **sister dream chaser** (favourite among your siblings and that favouritism surrounds you like a Colourful glorious coat). Your siblings resent you because they see it as unfair because you also have tendency knowingly or unknowingly of using it to taunt them.

In every kind of 'family' (whether a biological one, church family, business family), or a social friendship family, there will be someone who will stand out exceptionally and will be clothed with more favour by leaders and authorities in that family. **Sister dream chaser** will have a supernatural radical faith in where they are going and the heights they want to reach, which will annoy her **sister dream killer** that ultimately leads to the sibling rivalry.

You could also be the gifted one in your family who has big dreams; because somehow you recognize the greatness within you, and you have some revelation about your Purpose and Destiny.

And in your naivety, you share it with your **sister dream killer** boastfully and pridefully which adds to her resentment towards you. Inevitably your sister dream killer devices how to get you out of the way so she can take your place and enjoy your favour and take your "Colourful coat" which represents your Destiny.

You thereafter find yourself in abandonment, and your dreams for fulfilling your dreams are thrown in a pit, then in a prison and you go through all manner of calamities, injustices tests and trials. Yet ultimately and miraculously you survive to fulfil your Destiny but your sister dream killer thinks you are dead.

"He who digs a pit for his brother shall fall in it and he who sets up traps for others shall be caught in them." ~ **Ahiqar**

Your story is not over because you then encounter your **sister dream killer** whose life did not succeed and she never fulfilled her Purpose and has not yet entered her Destiny. So, you are left with the choice to either revenge or help her.

As **sister dream killer** will throw you and your dreams into a pit of abuse, abandonment and rejection seeking to kill your dreams but by God's grace you survive it all.

When this sibling rivalry occurs, there will inevitably be a separation between you and your dream killer sister. She thinks she has killed you and your dreams, yet you are very much alive and elsewhere fulfilling your Purpose and Destiny.

The right response to your **sister dream killer** (as and when you are reunited and tables have turned whereby you are the one with all the power and success) is to forgive her and be the bigger person, since despite her every wicked effort you survived and thrived.

Your ability to forgive is maturity. It shows you have a revelation that she had no power to kill you, your dreams or your Destiny and she never did.

As the **sister dream killer** in this scenario, you must not envy your **sister dreamer's** dreams. Instead, you should dream your own dreams discover your own Calling and Destiny and embark on fulfilling it. Trying to kill your sisters dream and Destiny will not give you any advantage because you will still end up without any dreams for yourself.

The fact that your sister has dreams, Calling and Destiny does not deny you yours, and the fact that she is favoured with a colourful coat does not mean that you will not be favoured and have a colourful coat if you sincerely desire and pursue it.

As **sister dreamer** you must be careful who you share your dreams with and also avoid showing off about the greatness that is within you. You must forgive every wrong that was done to you by your **sister dream killer** because in the process of trying to cause you harm, you went through a process that strengthened you that made you wiser. The process enabled you to discover and fulfil your Calling and Destiny, because the trials, tribulations and fiery furnaces, you went through empowered you as s Destiny vessel.

7. A LEPROSY PENALTY

(*Sister destiny climber vs side ladder holder*)

In any family, for every **Sister Destiny Climber** there should be a **Sister Ladder Holder**.

Sometimes the older and stronger or wiser or more experienced sibling in a family may play the role of protecting the younger and weaker one in the earlier years of life. She may even save the life of that younger one in several dangerous situations and protect that younger sibling from a lot of attacks, oppression or abuse from other people.

The stronger **sister ladder holder** begins to believe that, had it not been for her, that younger sister **Destiny climber** would not have made it this far.

So, this **sister ladder holder** may feel entitled and expect this **sister Destiny climber** to always owe her and be grateful and always consult her before making any decisions in her life. The protective spirit in the **sister ladder holder** turns into a manipulative controlling spirit overtime.

However, **sister Destiny climber** may end up becoming the chosen one, the successful prominent and more influential sibling (in whatever family context it is) and **sister ladder holder** is relegated to a back seat to a lower position of supporting, serving and following.

So, the rivalry arises when the **sister ladder holder** harshly judges the now successful and more influential sister **Destiny climber**. She criticizes her decisions without respect and with a view to undermining her influence. Herein lies the "leprosy penalty" which symbolizes the dire consequences that **sister ladder holder** will suffer as a result of dishonouring the leader in sister Destiny climber. Once someone is chosen in a leadership position, we must respect that leadership office whether that person is younger than us or whether we feel we helped them to get there.

Whereas a **sister Destiny climber** you are now the stronger one, you must take up that position without any apology (and even while you are grateful for what your **sister ladder holder** did for you). Nonetheless you must not let her undermine you and hinder you from fulfilling your Purpose and Destiny no matter how emotionally attached to her.

Your Purpose and Destiny is your life. It is the reason why you are alive and where a conflict arises between your emotional attachments to your siblings (in whatever family context) and your Purpose and Destiny, then you must choose your Purpose and Destiny over anyone and anything.

Where you are the **sister ladder holder** you must get the revelation that your **sister Destiny climber** (who you once helped and protected and who followed you like a puppy trusting your every advice and consulting you on every issue) has now matured and risen to heights of authority and influence that you must submit to humbly and respectively.

Remember that your assignment and Purpose is to actually remain submitted to that sibling as her Destiny helper as you bear her burdens and hold up her ladder faithfully until she fulfils her Destiny.

This scenario is similar to a **"Big sister syndrome"** where at the beginning as the little sister you may be at the bottom of the rank, (in the family or workplace, church, business, organization etc.) You are seen as insignificant and irrelevant, who is of no good and of no value, in comparison to your successful, famous, bigger sister. So, you more or less accept that position and you keep the gifts and talents that are within you in obscurity without expecting any recognition or accolades and without expecting to have any real impact on anyone or anywhere.

Whereas your **'big sister'** is preferred because of her outward appearance charisma value relevance position and status etc. She begins to adopt a big sister syndrome and, seeks to undermine and belittle you into nothingness and you may become so intimidated until you doubt your Purpose and Destiny thinking you are not worthy, and you remain in your big sister shadow.

Your "Veteran" big sister therefore gets shocked when that which was developing in obscurity (and the gifts and anointing within you that no one thought you had) suddenly manifests into the limelight and propels you into places even you never thought possible. The tables turn and you become the impactful influential and stronger one whether in the family organization, church, society or nation etc.

When tables turn, do not be dishonourable, or spend time confronting your "Veteran" big sister. The greatness within you will do it for you and if she cannot handle your greatness then it is her loss not yours. As far as it is practicably possible do not burn your bridges with your big sister who is also your Destiny helper as your ladder holder. Instead make peace and accord her the respect she deserves and show her your gratitude for all she has done for you but ensure to maintain boundaries where she does not intimidate or seek to control you. She must respect the leader in you and the office of the leader.

This sibling rivalry can also manifest itself in another common scenario where the stronger sibling seeks to lord it over the weaker sibling (whether due to age, finances, status, success, influence or any other strength). So, this is also a case of big sister and a little sister syndrome.

So just like the **sister Destiny climber** and the **sister ladder** rivalry, the "big sister/small sister syndrome" can be managed and carefully handled in a way that both sisters operate in mutual respect and they go on to fulfil their respective Calling and Destiny.

Destiny Questions to Ponder On

1. Have you ever been in a **Sister Hood Competition**, how did you handle yourself in the situation?

2. Have you ever been in a **Fattened Calf affair**, how did you handle yourself in the situation?

3. Have you ever been part of a **Legitimacy Legend**, how did you handle yourself in the situation?

4. Have you ever been in a **Birth Right Battle**, how did you handle yourself in the situation?

5. Have you ever been in a **Fatal Envy**, how did you handle yourself in the situation?

6. Have you ever been in a **Colourful Coat Contention**, how did you handle yourself in the situation?

7. Have you ever been part of a **Leprosy Penalty**, how did you handle yourself in the situation?

This Page Was Intentionally Left Blank

Chapter Six

MASTERING THE ART OF NEGOTIATION

Seeking Mutually Beneficial Outcomes in Your Relationships

Chapter Preview

1. *Be Purpose Driven, Not Power Driven*

2. *Leveraging on Merit, Not Mercy*

3. *Be Dignified, Not Desperate*

4. *Use your Brain power, Not your Beauty potency*

5. *By Purposeful Planning, Not Plotting*

6. *Be Assertive, Not Aggressive*

7. *Seal with Prayer not Presumption*

OPENING REMARKS

Mastering the art of negotiation helps to position you effectively at your place and sphere. Negotiation is an art, a skill, a creative style, a strategy, acquired through practice, application of certain principles. It is developing the skill, style and strategy for leveraging your position and getting past the notion that women don't ask.

Negotiating is not to dictate or demand but it implies a give, take and compromise where you explain your position, listen to the other side. It's a bargaining process whose outcome is for mutual benefit.

"We cannot negotiate with people who say what's mine is mine and what's yours is negotiable." ~ **John F. Kennedy**

In your journey to Destiny and as you seek to fulfil your Purpose, engage and interact with people at your sphere of assignment, you will definitely find yourself in situations where you need to negotiate. It could be for better pay and working terms in your organization, whether it is to have a bigger voice in your family's affairs. It could be in your business and entrepreneurial endeavours with your business partners. It could be within professional bodies with your professional colleagues or any other situation. You need to leverage and bargain for what is necessary for you to fulfil your Purpose and enter your Destiny.

Negotiating will require some level of emotional intelligence, social skills and people skills in order for it to be effective and beneficial.

We need to overthrow the common notion that women in the market place are disadvantaged when it comes to negotiation in the work place in terms of higher salaries, flexi hours, fair treatment at work or more help at home, more opportunities etc.

"Nice girls do not ask but smart women do" ~ **Lois P. Frankel**

We also need to overcome another common belief that women often don't know what they want to ask for or negotiate for. More critically that many women do not ask even when they know what they want.

Beware of the "**Tiara Syndrome**" where you work so hard and you keep your head down hoping somebody will notice and put a tiara on your head, without you asking for it. Some women have a wrong mind-set of thinking that they should not ask for what they are truly entitled to. Some feel it may not seem very christian or lady-like or it may make them look greedy and demanding. It is important to get rid of this mind-set and adopt the right negotiating skills.

"Hope is not a strategy" ~ **Sheryl Sandberg**

Some of the factors attributed to this tragic mind-set (where women don't ask for what they are entitled to) are fear, social inclinations, outdated traditions and repressive cultures, and the implications and responsibilities that come with getting what you have asked for. You will need to give more energy and hours and make more sacrifices, because additional powers and privileges always come with additional sacrifices, responsibilities, challenges and battles.

Many women also fear that climbing to a higher level may expose her weaknesses as she becomes visible, or she will become a burden and a liability if she fails to perform up to the required expectations. You must eradicate this fear of failure mentality.

"Let us never negotiate out of fear. But let us never fear to negotiate." **John F. Kennedy**

Factors such as cultural myths, traditions and social conditioning, self-effacing, under estimating yourself, and believing that nice girls don't ask (which is misinterpreting the word "nice") are all unfortunate hindrances and obstacles that many women face in their journey to Destiny and which you must resist and overcome.

Other factors are where women do not know why they want what they want. Having no clear Vision and goals, not knowing your Purpose and Place of Assignment and not knowing your market worth and value.

"The best move you can make in negotiation is to think of an incentive the other person hasn't even thought of – and then meet it." ~ **Eli Broad**

As women of Destiny, we need know how to change the way we negotiate so that we may negotiate more effectively. Some of the factors that may enhance our negotiating skills are knowing your person in terms of who you are, your value, your relevance, your skills and strengths. Discovering your Purpose, locating your sphere of assignment, identifying your relevant relationships and networks. Understanding and embracing the process you will need to undergo in your journey to Destiny. Establishing your principles, values and beliefs, and understanding exactly what you want and why you want it.

Some of the principles of negotiating effectively include making your negotiation Purpose driven and not power driven, using merit instead of pleading for mercy, being dignified instead of being desperate, using your brains instead of your beauty, your character instead of your charisma, using your sense of value and not sexual favours, careful planning as opposed to plotting, knowing your timing instead of arm twisting, applying wisdom instead of worldliness, being assertive instead of aggressive, having a right attitude as opposed to a wrong attitude and lastly approaching your negotiation with prayer and not presumption.

At the end of the day even after adopting all the requisite principles and skills of negotiation you may find that particular negotiations may fail. The test at that point will be how to surrender the situation. Accept to let it go, consider your alternatives and options. Ensure that you leave a door open to revisit the issues in the future without burning your bridges, damaging relationships permanently or discrediting yourself and soiling your reputation.

"Knowing when to walk away is wisdom, being able to do is courage, walking away with your head held high is dignity." Unknown

Always make sure that whatever you are negotiating for is something aligned to your Calling and Destiny.

1. BE PURPOSE DRIVEN, NOT POWER DRIVEN

"Purpose is the master of motivation and the mother of commitment"
~ Myles Munroe

When negotiating it is important that you align what you want with your Purpose and Destiny so that whatever you are asking for is geared towards empowering you to fulfil your Purpose and enter your Destiny.

Without discovering and knowing your Purpose you will not be able to negotiate correctly. Ask for what aligns with your Purpose, instead of making vain demands which are devoid of any meaning and Purpose. This is because whatever you are negotiating for (in whichever area of your life) should relate and align to the Destiny and Purpose you are seeking to fulfil.

Knowing your Purpose and using it as leverage will be more effective than trying to wield power that is not supported by any substance.

"Power is like being a lady... if you have to tell people you are, you aren't." ~ Margaret Thatcher

In other words, using force to get what you want without aligning what you want with the Purpose for which you want it is merely an ego trip.

"Your ego is your soul's worst enemy" Rusty Eric

- Know **what** you were created for, namely your Purpose so that what you are asking for should be a tool to enable you fulfil your Purpose, Vision and dream.
  "To begin to think with Purpose, is to enter the ranks of those strong ones who only recognize failure as one of the pathways to attainment." ~ James Allen
- Know **who** you are – even before you can know what your Purpose is or be effective in doing it, you must first define and understand your self-identity because it is only by being, that you can then embark on the doing.
  Knowing your self-identity entails understanding about what does and does not define you so that it is those factors that define you that will determine what you are negotiating for.

"It's not enough to have lived. We should be determined to live for something." ~ Winston S. Churchill

Where you are not clear about your Purpose upon which to base your negotiations, you may be tempted to name drop or use whatever power and authority at your disposal to control the situation and get your own way. Sometimes you may rely on political, social and economic power that you may have or other factors that give you influence. This means that ultimately if you do get your way, then it is more by blackmail as opposed to using the arts and skills of proper negotiation. Beware that you do not make negotiation about power.

Know, **where** (your Place of Assignment) the factors in your sphere of assignment will greatly affect what you want and what you are asking for. In fact, most of the negotiating you will do will be at your sphere of assignment. It is at your ordained sphere that you will find most of what you will require for Purposes of fulfilling your Destiny.

The various spheres of influence include politics and governance, business and economy, media, arts and entertainment, education, family and church. Knowing which sphere you have been called to influence and impact will enable you to know what you need and want for effectively impacting and influencing your sphere.

Once you know your sphere then you negotiate with relevance and understanding of what you need.

Knowing your strengths and weaknesses and the gaps you need to fill. Knowing the areas in which you are already advantaged, skilled and gifted. Knowing the areas in which you are disadvantaged and lacking in will enable you understand what you need to ask for and negotiate for. It will give you the necessary leverage to fulfil your Purpose and Destiny.

- Know your motivations and agendas is crucial in determining whether the reasons you are asking for something are credible and valid, selfless and others-oriented or purely self-serving and misguided.

Negotiate first with yourself before you come to the negotiating table. You must first come to terms with exactly what your deal breakers are, what your boundaries are and what principles and values will guide your negotiating and asking. This will enable you to be firm and clear and not easily manipulated and confused. It will also enable you to be flexible where need be.

"The greatest discovery of all times is that a person can change his future by merely changing his attitude." ~ Oprah Winfrey

During negotiation the attitude you adopt could either make or break the process and it could either strengthen or weaken your position. Have an open mind full of hope that the outcome will be mutually beneficial.

So having a positive attitude during the process as opposed to having a negative attitude is crucial in the success of the negotiations.

"Virtually nothing is impossible in this world if you just put your mind to it and maintain a positive attitude." ~ Lou Holtz

Avoid sulking or pouting, murmuring or complaining because such behaviour only points to your immaturity and lack of emotional intelligence. A good right attitude is contagious and it will create a healthy negotiating atmosphere.

"Each day, I come in with a positive attitude, trying to get better." ~ Stefon Diggs

A bad attitude always demonstrate immaturity and causes people not to trust you and to disrespect you. Your right and good attitude will earn you respect and honour and favour. So, watch your attitude because it's usually the first thing people notice about you.

"A bad attitude is like a burst tyre you cannot move on until you change it." ~ Unknown

A positive and right attitude creates a healthy atmosphere and enhances your ability and the other party's ability to be fair and reasonable as opposed to having a negative attitude which creates a toxic atmosphere which undermines your ability and the other party's ability to be fair and reasonable.

A positive attitude will lead to positive outcomes.

"Having a positive mental attitude that prompts you to expect favourable results is crucial" Unknown

2. LEVERAGING ON MERIT, NOT MERCY

"The most difficult thing in any negotiation, almost, is making sure that you strip it of the emotion and deal with the facts." ~ Howard Baker

What you are negotiating and asking for should ideally be based on what you know you are qualified and entitled to.

What you are getting should be based on merit as opposed to expecting that you be given something on the basis of people feeling sorry for you.

"I judge people based on their capability, honesty and merit." ~ Donald Trump

Negotiating on merit will make you credible and respectable as opposed to grovelling and acting desperate and needy, (which only discredits and weakens you in the eyes of the other party).

Believe that you are the answer and solution needed and that you are relevant and you have value to add. Be confident and believe that you deserve and are entitled, so get rid of any victim mentality and negotiate from a position of a victor.

You must approach the negotiating table with humility but confident and knowing that the other party is not doing you a favour because you are indeed entitled and qualified for what you are asking for.

"It seems to never occur to fools that merit and good fortune are closely united." ~ Johann Wolfgang von Goethe

Avoid invoking sympathy or pity either by your words, posture or demeanour. At the same time avoid adopting a hard arrogant stance that can be off-putting and repulsive and avoid pleas that reduce you and weaken your bargaining power.

In other words, do not expose your weaknesses in order to justify why you should be given what you are asking for. You must believe that those you are negotiating with need you more than you need them or at any rate you need each other equally.

Also be careful not to use your personal needs or wants to justify or cloud what you are really merited for, (for example, do not ask for an increased salary on the basis that you want to live in an affluent residential area which is expensive as opposed to negotiating for a salary based to your qualifications and good performance).

You must use your value as a negotiating tool, not your desires and wants. When you are valuable, you have the leveraging power when negotiating.

Your merit speaks to your credibility, so you must not exaggerate your meritocracy. As far as possible you should be credible and honest in selling yourself and your value because there is a thin line between giving yourself credit and over exaggerating and misrepresenting facts.

3. BE DIGNIFIED, NOT DESPERATE

Negotiating with dignity will make you credible and respectable as opposed to grovelling and acting desperate and needy, which only discredits and weakens you in the eyes of the other party.

Always ensure that as you negotiate you do so in a dignified and gracious manner even though firmly and confidently, be honourable and give honour and respect to all. Your dignified manner and posture will demonstrate your credibility and worth.

"I may lose many things in my life but if I lose my dignity, my honour, then I am lost" ~ *Unknown*

As a Woman of Destiny, dignity is one of your hallmarks and trademarks. As you conduct your affairs, do so in a dignified manner which means being worthy of honour and respect composed without any erratic behaviour that shows desperation or a lack of self-control. Instead, be gracious because there is great power when you operate in grace.

Therefore, when you enter the negotiating space, your posture and demeanour should be that of a Woman in control who appears reasonable (without drama and unruly emotions) and it is for these reasons those you are negotiating with will respect you and trust you.

4.   USE YOUR BRAIN POWER, NOT YOUR BEAUTY POTENCY

"Brains is better than beauty, beauty fades away but brains will not, beauty depends upon the eyes of the beholder whereas brain will be accepted as universal criterion." ~ *Gautam Thapa*

When negotiating always backup your arguments with solid facts and sound reasoning, and statistics etc. in order to give your position credibility.

Outward beauty is a superficial tool for negotiating and it is also manipulative. It is deceptive to rely on it because it is hard to maintain. Beauty fades and ultimately you will lose whatever you gained using your beauty and outward appearance. Hence the reason you should use something more permanent, credible and solid like your intellect, knowledge, wisdom, education and your brains.

It is true that sometimes one may have beauty as well as brains. Combined the two factors may actually give you favour and enhance your negotiating abilities, which is quite in order provided that you did not set out to use your beauty on its own.

"Beauty and brains, pleasure and usability they should go hand in hand" ~ Donald A. Norman

For example, there are some service industries where one is chosen according to their outward physical appearance like their beauty. At that point her beauty is definitely leverage and she can easily negotiate for what she is entitled to, (where her beauty is a value add to that business or industry) but not as a deceptive, manipulative tool where you take advantage of the weaknesses of others especially the opposite sex, who may compromise values in the process. As honourable respectable women of Destiny, we must never push other people towards immorality, sin or any other wrong doing by using our outward beauty.

However, over time that beauty will fade in the eyes of the beholder and consequently also your value in that industry and sector and your bargaining power will become weakened.

"Character is the real foundation of all worthwhile success." ~ *John Hays Hammond*

It is therefore always advisable to use your brains in terms of IQ and EQ because those are long lasting and they only get enhanced over time not faded.

Beauty may take you there but it is brains and character that will keep you there.

"Knowledge will give you power, but character respect." ~ **Bruce Lee**

In addition, use character not charisma when negotiating because solid character is consistent behaviour, words and actions. Let your character go ahead of you, because it will give you credibility and integrity and earn you respect.

Negotiate with respectful appeal but not with flamboyant charisma because that would be using personal magnetism and charm (arousing popular devotion and enchantment which may not have substance).

"Good character improves every aspect of a person's life." ~ John C. Maxwell

The main difference between character and charisma, is that character focuses on the inner qualities which make up an individual and draws others to you due to those qualities. While charisma deals with the external magnetism which an individual can use to draw the attention of others. So, charisma can be a counterfeit for character because it is an outward appearance yet character is what is truly within but charisma is superficial.

Sometimes during negotiations, you may be tempted to use your sex appeal which is basically manipulation. It will lose you respect in the end even if it gets you what you want temporarily.

Instead, you should use common sense and logical arguments to explain why you should get what you are asking for because common sense demonstrates your maturity and decency.

5. BY PURPOSEFUL PLANNING, NOT PLOTTING

"To achieve great things, two things are needed: a plan and not quite enough time." ~ Leonard Bernstein

When negotiating you need to prepare carefully in advance by researching and having all your information at hand, knowing your facts well and also knowing all you need to know about the organization and business of the party you are negotiating.

Also, you need to know the requirements, values, beliefs and character of the persons you are negotiating with. Knowledge is empowering and once you are equipped with it, you'll be able to strengthen your bargaining position.

All the scheming and plotting in the world will not result in anything lasting or true. When evil people plot, good people must plan. Sitting at a negotiation table without having adequate preparation and planning will only show you as a disorganized person who has no clarity of intention as to exactly what she wants which will undermine your position.

"By failing to prepare, you are preparing to fail." ~ **Benjamin Franklin**

Avoid scheming and plotting or adopting any under handedness. Those are the tactics used by people who do not have the merit or qualifications to deserve and be entitled to what they are asking for. On your part, you have what it takes so you can deal honestly and confidently and above board.

Pro.16:3 – *"Commit your works to the LORD, and your thoughts will be established."*

Timing is everything. Discern the right timing for you to initiate negotiations. Ask yourself whether it's the right timing for you for the other party and for the organization because moving prematurely will sabotage and deny you getting what you would have gotten if the timing was right.

Synchronizing and syncopating are crucial elements in the art of negotiation, because ensuring that all things are aligned in terms of timing, planning etc. will give the negotiation a higher chance of success.

When you move prematurely before time, you may end up arm twisting the other party and pushing them into a corner to make decisions that they are not prepared to make. Even where you may get your way, you will have gotten it by a form of blackmailing, pressuring and undue duress and by having taken advantage of the other party's lack of option which obviously weakened their position.

"There is timing in everything. Timing in strategy cannot be mastered without a great deal of practice. ~ **Miyamoto Musashi**

For example, where as an accountant you seek to negotiate for salary increment, and it is the time for the audit, and the tax authorities are on the organizations back, then that kind of negotiating is tantamount to hidden threats and blackmail.

"Timing is everything; when you are really ready for it, it will come." ~ *Mandy Hale*

6. BE ASSERTIVE, NOT AGGRESSIVE

"Assertiveness is your ability to act in harmony with your self-esteem without hurting others" ~ **Unknown**

You don't have to be aggressive to be empowered.

Do not be intimidated neither should you intimidate. In addition, you should avoid undermining any proposals or counter proposals from the other party by ridiculing them. Likewise, you should not allow or entertain them ridiculing or undermining your proposals or counter proposals.

Never ever threaten or use threatening language or posture and avoid misguided aggression. Choose instead to use meekness, which is a sign of maturity and strength and not weakness because you are exercising the power and authority within you maturely and with restraint.

"Calmness is more influential than words." ~ Thomas Caryle

Remember that not everyone can handle your greatness so you must put the other party at ease by using wisdom so that your greatness and awesomeness does not become offensive and derail the negotiation.

Aggressiveness shows that you are insecure, ill-mannered and disrespectful. It displays feelings of anger, hostility, violence, readiness to attack, forcefulness and seeking to dominate and control the other party (because you are either insecure about who you are and whether you deserve what you are asking for). It shows you are fearful of losing and hence the reason you become toxic and unruly.

"Aggression is the first step on the slippery slope to selfishness and chaos" ~ Anne Campbell

On the other hand, assertiveness is merely being firm politely, expressing and articulating your position respectfully. It does not mean disrespecting or ignoring the feelings of others, it means that you are willing to stand up for yourself fairly without undermining the position of others.

"The basic difference between being assertive and being aggressive is how your words and behaviours affect the rights and the well-being of others." Sharon Antony Bower

7. SEAL WITH PRAYER NOT PRESUMPTION

"Our prayers may be awkward. Our attempts may be feeble. But since the power of prayer is in the one who hears it and not in the one who says it, our prayers do make a difference." ~ Max Lucado

As a Woman of Destiny, every venture and endeavour in your life should be covered in fervent prayer for a successful outcome.

Phil.4:6 – *"Be anxious for nothing, but in everything by prayer and supplication, with thanksgiving, let your requests be made known to God"*

Consequently, as you prepare and enter the negotiation process you must ensure to have committed all the issues in prayer. Praying for a healthy atmosphere, a favourable outcome and for the safeguarding of those relationships, (so that they will not be prejudiced and damaged in the process). As you apply the principles of Purpose driven, merit, character, assertion, wisdom etc., let prayer be the foundation as well as the seal.

Your prayers must be in conjunction with your thorough research, prudent preparation and skilled presentation.

Misguided presumption is dangerous because it leads to disappointments, shame and loss.

"Ignorance is the mother of presumption" ~ Marie De Gournay

Prayer on the other hand is based on clean promises that God has given you in His word so you can pray and stand on those promises as you negotiate.

Proverbs 21:1 – "The King's heart is in the hand of the Lord, Like the rivers of water; He turns it wherever He wishes."

This is because above every human authority, is a divine authority who you can appeal to persuade the human authority.

"True prayer is neither a mere mental exercise nor a vocal performance. It is far deeper than that - it is spiritual transaction with the Creator of Heaven and Earth." ~ Charles Spurgeon

Your prayer effort should include your trusted prayer partners and intercessors who are your burden carriers and they will therefore be able to push in prayer on your behalf even where you are too stressed and nervous to do it yourself.

"To be a Christian without prayer is no more possible than to be alive without breathing." ~ **Martin Luther**

The opposite of prayer is to be overconfident and presumptuous. It is to assume that you will be able to succeed without any divine assistance or support. Such presumptions will always end up backfiring into disillusionment.

Never confuse arrogant presumption with praying boldly.

There is a difference.

"Wisdom is the power to put our time and our knowledge to the proper use." ~ Thomas J. Watson

When negotiating and having prepared yourself adequately then the next imperative is to employ a lot of wisdom in your approach, words and responses so as to establish a fair playing ground and to gain some favour with those you are negotiating with.

James 1:5 – *"If any of you lacks wisdom, let him ask of God, who gives to all liberally and without reproach, and it will be given to him."*

Do not use wiliness that demonstrates craftiness, shrewdness, deception, foxiness and slyness, to get your own way.

"Deception may give us what we want for the present, but it will always take it away in the end" ~ **Rachel Hawthorne**

Avoiding emotional outbursts and reactions and instead using wise restraints, intuition and calmness and basically being winsome which means endearing and pleasant as opposed to being ugly, irrational and harsh.

Be authentic and sincere and apply your verbal and relational skills by using the right words. Maintain a calm gentle spirit, get rid of the fight mode but assert yourself firmly, boldly and courageously.

Adopting and mastering these simple arts of negotiation at your place and sphere will ensure that you achieve your goals for fulfilling your Destiny. You retain your dignity, relationships, credibility and favour with all those you will constantly negotiate with there.

The key is to use a win-win collaborative strategy and approach so that as far as it is practicably possible you get a mutually beneficial outcome where all parties are accommodated. Your ability to build others as you build yourself is a master key to fulfilling your Destiny.

Destiny Questions to Ponder On

1. *Have you ever been in a negotiation, where you used **Power instead of Purpose** and if so, what was the outcome?*

2. *Have you ever been in a negotiation, where you used **mercy instead of merit** charisma instead of character and if so, what was the outcome?*

3. *Have you ever been in a negotiation, where you adopted **desperation instead of dignity** and if so, what was the outcome?*

4. *Have you ever been in a negotiation, where you used your **beauty instead of your brains** sex instead of sense and if so, what was the outcome?*

5. *Have you ever been in a negotiation, where you **plotted instead of planning** and timing and if so, what was the outcome?*

6. *Have you ever been in a negotiation, where you used wiliness instead of wisdom **aggression instead of assertiveness** and if so, what was the outcome?*

7. *Have you ever been in a negotiation, where you used **presumptions instead of prayer** and if so, what was the outcome?*

This Page Was Intentionally Left Blank

Chapter Seven

THE SPICE GIRLS
OF A DESTINY GAL

Appreciating The Power of Female Friendships

Chapter Preview

1. *Your Garlic Spice Girl is your Rock*

2. *Your Salt Spice Girl is your Truth*

3. *Your Ginger Spice Girl is your Bodyguard*

4. *Your Mint Spice Girl is your Hero*

5. *Your Cinnamon Spice Girl is your Cheerleader*

6. *Your Nutmeg Spice Girl is your Carefree Spirit*

7. *Your Sweet and Sour Girl is your Mirror*

OPENING REMARKS

"Womens' networks are a necessary part of life. A mixture of empathy and brainstorming can move mountains." ~ Hazel Hawke

Your women friends and confidants are like spices because they flavour, season, and colour your life in various ways. Their influence reflects the different aspects of yourself, complimenting your characteristics and often bringing out the best in you. So that instead of being bland and dull you become tasteful and palatable, and all together spicy and well-Seasoned for Destiny. Most importantly each of these women friends should have a positive impact in propelling you in fulfilling your Calling and Destiny.

"The circles of women around us weave invisible nets of love that carry us when we are weak and sing with us when we are strong."
~ SARK

Women are each other's support. Girlfriends have a distinctive way of reading emotions so they are the backbone of your support system.

"The best kind of friendships are the fierce lady friendships where you aggressively believe in each other, defend each other and think that the other deserves the world." Unknown

It is sad that often female friendships will be portrayed negatively and criticized for being toxic and full of drama and conflict. This is an exaggeration intended to cause fear and apprehension among women and to hinder them from bonding.

"Abandon the cultural myth that all female friendships must be toxic or competitive." ~ Roxane Gay

Without women friendships in your life, you will become lonely, isolated and with pent up emotions with no one to vent to. Even your closest male friend like your spouse comes nowhere near the comfort that true female friendships will give you.

The loneliest women in the world are those without close women friends. Women are meant to bond and don't let anyone tell you otherwise. Unbreakable female bonds can solidify your happiness and uphold you in your journey to Destiny.

"A friend is someone who stands by you when you encounter a difficult situation, and is always there to celebrate your achievement." ~**Unknown**

Women support each other and cheer each other on. It is often said that behind every successful Woman is a tribe of other women who have her back.

"True friends are like diamonds - bright, beautiful, valuable and always in style." ~ **Nicole Richie**

Whatever decade you may be in (whether in your trendy twenties, thriving thirties, fortified forties, fabulous fifties, splendid sixties, serene seventies, elegant eighties, or even your noble nineties and beyond) it may be necessary for you to identify (if you have not already done so) some women who are your "Closest Spice Girls", from among your women friends. Ascertain the Purpose why each one of them is in your life and the value each one of them is bringing into your life so as to enable you relate and respond to each one of them appropriately.

In addition, you must ascertain your own Purpose and role in each of your Spice Girl's life and ensure that there is some value you are also adding to each one of them.

"Never ignore a person who loves you, cares for you and misses you, because one day you might wake up from your sleep and realize that, you lost the moon while counting the stars." ~ **John O'Callaghan**

It is possible that you may identify more than 7 types of Spice Girl friendships. From observation these are seven types that stand out.

The Garlic Spice represents your Strong Spice Girl who is your **Rock**, Salt Spice represents your Transparent Spice Girl who is your **Truth**, Ginger Spice represents your Protective Spice Girl who is your **Body Guard**, Mint Spice represents your Admirable Spice Girl who is your **Hero**, Cinnamon Spice represents your Cheerful Supportive Spice Girl, who is your **Cheerleader**, Nutmeg Spice represents your Spontaneous Spice Girl who is your **Carefree Spirit** and Sweet and Sour Sauce represents your Twin Spice Girl who is your **Mirror**.

1. YOUR GARLIC SPICE GIRL IS YOUR ROCK

This girl will stand with you through thick and thin, instilling strength and fortitude. She is careful because like garlic, her breath of strength can be offensive when you just need to be weak for a while and recover from a fall back that left you depleted. So, she balances between allowing you a weakness grace period and uplifting you so that you don't stay there too long.

"You can't be strong all the time, sometimes you just need to be alone and let your tears out." **Unknown**

The garlic spice has many benefits and contains compounds with medicinal properties, it is highly nutritious with very few calories. It is commonly believed that it can combat sickness including the common cold, reduce high blood pressure, improve cholesterol levels which ultimately lowers the risk of heart disease.

It is also believed that garlic supplements can boost the functions of the immune system, improve athletic performance, detoxify heavy metals in the body and improve your bone health. We can therefore infer that beyond the fact that the garlic spice adds a delicious flavour to foods, it has many other benefits.

The common cold comes about as a result of a compromised immune system so it could symbolize that your **Garlic spice friend,** helps you to boost your immunity so you can withstand those subtle attacks that keep you sniffing and miserable.

Reducing blood pressure and improving cholesterol levels (that helps to avoid the risk of heart disease) can symbolize that your **Garlic spice girl,** helps to strengthen your heart against the various challenges, frustrations, etc. that will come against you in your journey to Destiny. This friend strengthens you against despondency and hopelessness.

The detoxifying effect of the garlic spice could symbolize that your **Garlic spice girl,** helps you to release emotional and mental toxins that may often weaken you like anger, bitterness, offence, etc.

The power in the garlic to improve your athletic performance and bone health could symbolize that your **Garlic spice girl,** helps you to remain strong in running your race to Destiny. She helps to keep your inner resolve strong symbolizing your bone health.

And lastly the high nutrition but few calories in the garlic spice could symbolize that your **Garlic spice girl** helps you to feed on those things that strengthen you (like having a positive mind-set, pure emotions, and a godly outlook). She strengthens you emotionally, mentally and spiritually and to eliminate those things that weaken you (like a negative mind-set, toxic emotions and ungodliness).

So, garlic the spice is good medicinally, as it increases the overall health, and your **Garlic spice girl** is good for you because she represents one who helps you to remain strong and wholesome for your journey to Destiny.

"Keep your head high and your heart strong." ~ **Unknown**

This **Garlic spice girl** edifies and uplifts you when you are down or undergoing storms, tests and trials.

"A good friend is one who understands your strengths and weaknesses and still cherishes you for who you are." ~ Unknown

Your **Garlic spice girl** demonstrates real loving concern for you, offers you an empathetic ear. She affirms you by reminding you of all your strengths, gifts, talents etc. She inspires you towards what is positive, and she remains a consistent source of hope.

"You should surround yourself with relationships that encourage, inspire you and believe in your dreams." ~ Unknown

The good impact that this **Garlic spice girl** has on your Purpose and Destiny is undeniable, because as you encounter those hard seasons, she helps you to keep going. She is your rock who is graced and anointed to strengthen and encourage you with the right words and advice.

None of your other spice girls may be so graced to strengthen you. Instead, they may only end up loading you with guilt and shame for feeling weak. Their words and advice will come out all wrong, but your **Garlic spice girl** knows exactly how to balance her role in your life.

Garlic flavours and seasons food tastefully, and so does your **Garlic spice girl.**

2.   YOUR SALT SPICE GIRL IS YOUR TRUTH

This girl will tell you as it is, to keep you grounded and balanced…. Yet she is cautious not to hurt you with the raw hard truth. She weighs and measures it sensitively, so that she can avoid over-salting the issue (so as not to make the truth unpalatable).

"The truth is like salt. Men want to taste a little but too much makes everyone sick." ~ Joe Abercrombie

Salt is intended to add taste and symbolizes purity because of its colour. It is considered rare and sacred. So too your **Salt spice friend** is rare and precious, and hard to find. Hold on to her dearly and be grateful for her because she will often help you avoid aborting your Destiny.

Trust starts with truth and ends with truth and your salt friend who tells you the truth is one you can trust.

"Salt seasons, purifies, preserves, someone ought to remind us that salt also irritates." ~ **Vance Havner**

Just like salt is scared, your **Salt spice friend** therefore encourages you to embrace sacred things of the life that are pure and that keep you from evil and misfortune. Salt is a preservative, meaning that truth preserves and keeps you intact, likewise your **Salt spice girl** helps to preserve you for your call and Destiny by telling you the truth that you need to hear.

Salt is able to heal wounds even though in the process it stings painfully, meaning that your **Salt spice girl** will tell you the truth that will heal any of your mistakes and bad choices even though the healing process is painful.

Allow your **Salt spice friend** to dish out tough love to you and preserve you for your Destiny. Do not push her away just because the truth sometimes hurts.

Proverbs 27:5-6 - *"Open rebuke is better than love carefully concealed. Faithful are the wounds of a friend, but the kisses of an enemy are deceitful."*

In the natural, too much intake of salt can dehydrate your body (i.e., to dry up your body) which can lead to hypertension and ultimately to strokes and heart attacks. This could symbolize that overloading and ambushing someone with the hard raw truth that is painful without sensitivity. It can drain them and cause severe emotional heartache and panic and leave them extremely discouraged, overwhelmed and depleted.

Yet failure (in the natural) to take in sufficient salt can lead to a shortage of sodium. This leads to being over hydrated because of the intake of too much water known as "water intoxication" which is not good for the body.

This could symbolize that your **Salt spice girl** is good for you because by telling you the truth sensitively, she helps you to prevent being intoxicated with false assumptions and wrong conclusions that come with not knowing the real truth on an issue and thereby causing you to make wrong choices and decisions.

We all need at least one forthright, unabashedly honest and "bossy friend" in our lives. This friend doesn't say things to wound or cause drama, but she calls you out when you're trying to lie to yourself and we love her for it.

"A friend is someone who knows all about you and still loves you."
~ **Elbert Hubbard**

Your **Salt spice girl** is crucial in helping you remain accountable, honest and on the straight path as your journey to your Destiny.

However, and as a gentle caution, beware of any of your other friends, (who are not anointed and graced to be your salt friend). This is because in their zeal to help you, they can wound you and crush you by purporting to tell you the truth (without weighing or measuring it sensitively). Such friends will not know how to measure the salt and in the process, they will sting you and risk paralyzing you with pain.

That's why you must learn to sieve your spice girls and know who among them you will give access to which areas of your life, depending on the gracing upon each and the value and specific role each is intended to play in your life.

So, when you sense that the wrong spice girl (not graced to tell you the truth) is seeking to do so, quickly shut that door and only allow in the one anointed and graced for that role.

3. YOUR GINGER SPICE GIRL IS YOUR BODYGUARD

This girl will protect and cover you from every attack and shame… Yet she is careful to observe appropriate boundaries, lest she suffocates and begins to "own" you and shut you out from other valuable relationships in the guise of protecting you.

"True friendship isn't about being there when it is convenient, it's about being there when it's not." **Unknown**

The ginger spice is often used to treat loss of appetite and many stomach ailments so in a way it usually symbolizes your "womb" where you conceive your Visions, dreams and Purposes.

In the natural, the ginger spice in its root form is said to be a powerful weapon in the fight against cancer because of an active compound called Gingerol that is found within ginger, that has cancer fighting abilities.

Your **Ginger spice girl** could symbolize that she has an ability to help you fight and guard against those internal destructive things within you, that hinder you from effectively fulfilling your call and Destiny (such as self-doubt, fear, self-sabotage, victim syndrome etc.) She protects you from things and people around you that ignite and trigger those destructive elements within you.

The ginger spice also acts as an anti-inflammatory (treats and reduces harmful swelling), by lowering blood sugar (maintaining proper blood sugar levels), settle an upset stomach, curb nausea etc. This can symbolize that your **Ginger spice girl** is good for you because she helps you to avoid getting inflamed or swollen with anger or uncontrolled emotions. She helps you to balance your hormonal mood swings and remain self-controlled. She also protects you and helps you to guard against the attacks on your Visions and dreams while they are still in your "womb". She helps you calm your nerves when your emotions begin to rage and threaten to go out of control. In other words, she protects you from your own destructive patterns of behaviour etc.

A **Ginger spice friend** has sharp discernment and is able to analyse and see through the people around you who are seeking to deceive and misuse you, so she cautions you and protects from you from such.

The ginger spice is also often associated with limitless prosperity. This could symbolize that your **Ginger spice girl**, will protect and guard you against greed or unethical dealings in your wealth creation. Also, from those who may seek to steal from you and interfere with your wealth and resources.

This spice is also usually associated with diversity in personality. Symbolizing that your **Ginger spice girl** will protect and cover you from the diverse aspects of your character that may often put you in trouble. By covering and protecting you she ensures that you walk cautiously towards fulfilling your Purpose and Destiny. She is your fighter, protector and bodyguard from both yourself and from others.

Proverbs 17:17 – *"A friend loves at all times, and a brother is born in adversity."*

A good bodyguard friend understands situations very well and is able to discern your moments of crisis and the threats and dangers facing you. She has good judgment about how to diffuse a situation or crisis whether a scandal, an attack etc. and is committed in protecting you fiercely.

"Good friends are like stars, you don't always see them but you know they are always there." ~ **Christy Evans**

4. YOUR MINT SPICE GIRL IS YOUR HERO

This girl is the one who can do no wrong in your eyes and who inspires and calls out your deepest potentials as you aspire to climb higher and emulate her. Yet every hero has her weaknesses and your failure to humanize this girl may cause you great disillusionment and disappointment when you eventually realize that she is also human.

"How important it is for us to recognize and celebrate our heroes and she-roes" ~ **Maya Angelou**

The Mint spice is said to contain high levels of antioxidants promoting and maintaining youthfulness and it is also often used for fresh breath. Your time with your **Mint spice girl,** will be a time of cleansing and purifying and eliminating everything in you that is baggage and self-imposed limitations which hinder you from moving on in your Calling and Destiny. She also symbolizes refreshment, inspiration and growth, emotionally, mentally, spiritually and socially etc.

Therefore, your **Mint spice friend** brings a lot of freshness into your life in terms of ideas and Visions as she inspires you, and provokes you to unleash your full potential and greatness.

We all need friends we can bounce ideas off with (whether it's on major or minor issues about career, business, family, our Calling, dating, marriage etc.) It is healthy to get our emotions and thoughts out.

A good spring board friend won't come back to us with the one "right" answer, but will throw different ideas out there which will help us reach our own conclusions. Sometimes, we need to work it out for ourselves, but not by ourselves. A friend who asks things like, "how do you feel about that?" or "what are your options?" can provide just what we need in those moments.

Your **Mint Spice Girl** includes your mentors, role models, your coaches, or any person whose success or behaviour serves as an example for you. Someone who shares her experiences in terms of both successes and failures to teach and guide you, so that you can stand and take charge of your Purpose and Destiny.

"A lot of people have gone further than they thought they could because someone else thought they could." Zig Ziglar

Your **Mint spice girl** is a key helper in empowering and equipping you to fulfil your Destiny. Respect and guard the value in this spice girl, because even though she may not be so much older than you (or even where she may be younger than you), she's been there, done that and even "bought the T-shirt."

5. YOUR CINNAMON SPICE GIRL IS YOUR CHEERLEADER

"A good cheerleader is not measured by the height of her jumps but by the span of her spirit." Unknown

Usually this is a mentee-turned-friend or a younger woman, who sees you as "the best thing since sliced bread". She admires and sings your praises and cheers you on. Even though she may not have the capacity to coach you when you miss the ball, suffice she will keep you alert, awake and vibrant by her cheerfulness and encouragement.

"Friends are like your back bone; they are always there when you need support." ~ **Unknown**

In the natural, the cinnamon spice has some medicinal benefits that help your body fight infections and to repair tissue damage. This could symbolize that your **Cinnamon spice girl**, helps you to overcome negative and harmful influences that come to derail and distract you from your Calling and Destiny. She also helps you to recover when those negative and harmful influences actually cause you damage.

The Cinnamon spice is a combination of several spices symbolizing the need for diversity as well as union at the same time. Cinnamon is a spice often sprinkled onto beverages like coffee, tea, hot chocolate or used in desserts and puddings, to lift the flavour and give energy.

It therefore symbolizes and represents the sweet and the light added to things that lift you up and comfort you when you are down. Your **Cinnamon spice girl** therefore affirms you and lifts you in the midst of all the tough times, keeping you from drowning in the dreariness of life.

She is your enthusiastic and vocal supporter who raises your spirit, with her positive attitude that is infectious.

"True friends help you find important things when you have lost them; your smile; your hope and your courage." ~ **Doe Zantamata**

Sometimes we just want someone who will say nice things to us, a friend who is always positive, smiling and ready to tell you that you look good, and that you are enough.

The journey to fulfilling your Calling and Destiny is tough and rough enough and when times get heavy and overwhelming, we need a cheerleader so we don't give up and quit.

Your cheerleader **Cinnamon spice Girl** will never say a depressing or discouraging word to you or something distressful or difficult for you to hear. She provides a soft and safe place for you to land when you feel overwhelmed.

"Surround yourself with people who see your value and remind you of it." ~ **Unknown**

However always remember that your cheerleader's role is to cheer you up and remind you that you are well able and that you are the best in your field, so that you spring up and continue to fulfil your Purpose and Destiny.

However, you must be careful to remember that as much as your cheerleader may cheer you and help you only see the bright and positive side of your life, you must be wise enough to remember that life is not all roses and that's where your other spice girls come in like your truth etc. to help you have a balanced perspective.

Your role is to impact your cheerleader and also equip her and propel her to grow by sharing your life experiences which will encourage her and even admire you more.

6. YOUR NUTMEG SPICE GIRL IS YOUR CAREFREE SPIRIT

This girl will flow easily without heaviness and stress, allowing you to be a spontaneous carefree spirit of impulse when you need to be, to throw caution to the wind and push your boundaries to their limit… Yet she may not be strong enough to stop you when you begin to veer dangerously on the edge of reason and responsibility, so you must remain alert enough around your nutty **Nutmeg spice friend.**

Being a free spirit does not mean abandoning everyone or everything, it means being less bound by strict rules and regulations and allowing yourself to relax in some of your decisions and actions as long as they do not prejudice your Calling and Destiny.

"Some people arrive and make such a beautiful impact on your life; you can barely remember what life was like without them." ~ **Anna Taylor**

The nutmeg spice can be used to make all types of sauces meaning it is adaptable and open to be used in different ways. Nutmeg sometimes symbolizes good fortune and good times.

This means that your **Nutmeg spice friend** (though "nutty") adds a lot of joy and laughter into your life. She enables you to see the flip side of things so that you are not overwhelmed by the seriousness and heaviness of life because sometimes you have to laugh at yourself and at situations.

The nutmeg spice though small in size has some medicinal benefits like making you vibrant and energetic and boosting your mood and it has been claimed that it may have some significant antidepressant effects.

This **Nutty spice girl** allows you to be yourself, without putting any pressure on you about anything. She frees you to process things until you are ready to share them.

Close friends are true treasures, sometimes they know us better than we know ourselves. With gentle honesty they are there to guide us, support us, to share laughter and our tears. Their presence reminds us that we are never really alone.

Sometimes we simply don't want to talk about it, whatever it is. We aren't ready. It's too painful or too embarrassing. The greatest girlfriends know when silence is indeed golden and they make it easy for us; they listen and they don't ask. In return, we do the same for them, even if we have to bite our lip or pretend, we don't see and hear something that we do see or hear.

Sometimes the most empathy one girl can express to another, comes in the hush of quietness.

"Silence is a true friend who never betrays." ~ **Confucius**

The beauty of a **Nutty Spice friend** is that she draws you away from political correctness, so you can see things from a less serious perspective and think outside the box and be more creative. She brings out the "diva scent" in you in a good way and in different styles.

Fulfilling your Purpose and Destiny will sometimes require you to step out of the box of conventionality and be unfiltered.

7. YOUR SWEET AND SOUR GIRL IS YOUR MIRROR

In life, you should have a friend who is like a mirror and shadow. A mirror doesn't lie, and a shadow doesn't leave. She gets your every joke and finishes your every sentence... You share deep interests with her and are passionate about the same things… Yet those very similarities and commonalities will cause you to often feel suffocated and miss your own sense of individuality… Yet when you withdraw from her, you begin to miss her.

"The mirror is my best friend because when I cry it never laughs." ~ **Charlie Chaplin**

Your **Mirror spice girl** is often a true reflection and depiction of yourself than your own blood siblings. She reflects the kind of person you are, reflecting back your fears, flaws, insecurities and strengths in the most comforting way. In life you don't need a tall mirror but rather a long-standing friend. She knows your good sides and your bad ones and you pick up habits from each other as you grow together.

"A good friend holds up the mirror to show you your heart." ~ Unknown

The advantage of this **Mirror spice girl** friend is that she is able to help you as you fulfilly our Purpose and Destiny by virtue of knowing you so well. When we get stuck, she knows how to pull you out of the mud and how to motivate you.

However, you must be cautious with a **Mirror spice friend**, that you don't lose your individuality or become over dependent on her because ultimately, you alone has the responsibility for fulfilling your Destiny.

Sweet and sour sauce is exactly that. It tastes both sweet and sour at the same time, but instead of it being unpalatable, it ironically blends well and has a pleasant taste. Your relationship with this **Mirror spice friend** will have its rosy fragrances and its prickly thorns at the same time. This makes it quite paradoxical, because while you appear to be identical, inseparable twins, yet at the same time, you are each a very separate individual.

"Your mirror spice girl and you are very similar so you easily resonate." ~ Unknown

Through your **Mirror spice girl's** life, you can see what is right and what is wrong, even in your own life.

Conversely you should be your own mirror and your own best friend. Be a mirror for yourself, so that you can also stand independently and master the act of self-encouragement and self-motivation. Even when none of your spice girls are there, ultimately the responsibility of fulfilling your Purpose and Destiny lies squarely on you.

What your spice girls do, is to add to what you have already built and established in your life. They help you put issues in perspective. They are your truth, your strength, your bodyguard, your cheerleader and mirror etc. Each adding a different spice and each playing a very significant role in your life.

Patricia Leavy in her article *The Seven Codes of Female Relationships* says, ***"Women often have friendships and each type is based on specific patterns of interpersonal communication."***

Learning to accommodate the shortcomings in each of your Spice Girls is important in enabling you to also appreciate your own weaknesses and shortcomings. It helps you understand that ultimately it is the goodwill towards one another that matters as none of us is perfect.

In conclusion, as you embark on identifying your Spice Girls, remember that, the criteria is to weigh their input and influence in your life. Ensure that it is positive and valuable, rather than being negatively intrusive and overbearing. Keep in mind however that as necessary and valuable as these friendships are, ultimately, the responsibility for the choices and decisions you make regarding your Destiny lies with you.

Also remember that you are someone's salt spice girl and truth, someone's Ginger Spice Girl and bodyguard, someone's mint spice girl and hero, Someone's garlic spice girl and rock, someone's Cinnamon Spice Girl and cheerleader, Someone's nutmeg spice girl and carefree spirit and someone's sweet and sour sauce girl and mirror. Understanding your role and input in each of your spice girls is crucial so that you can propel that spice girl to fulfil her Calling and Destiny.

Your spice girls' relationships are Destiny relationships that will be a two-way traffic and mutually beneficial.

Destiny Questions To Ponder On

1. Which other aspects of friendship stand out in a **salt spice** friend?

2. Which other aspects of friendship stand out in a **garlic spice** friend?

3. Which other aspects of friendship stand out in a **ginger spice** friend?

4. Which other aspects of friendship stand out in a **nutmeg spice** friend?

5. Which other aspects of friendship stand out in a **mint spice** friend?

6. Which other aspects of friendship stand out in a **cinnamon spice** friend?

7. Which other aspects of friendship stand out in a **mirror** friend?

Chapter Eight

THE SUSPECT SUITORS OF A DESTINY WOMAN

The Relationship Dilemmas that Come in Choosing a Destiny Spouse

Chapter Preview

1. **The Wolf in Sheep's Clothing**

   (When You Have Conflicting Values)

2. **The Serial Deal Chaser**

   (When He Has a Breadwinner Deficiency Syndrome)

3. **The Golden Heir and the Bearded Baby**

   (When He is a Mama's Boy)

4. **The Superstar**

   (When You are His Trophy not His True Love)

5. **The Silver And Golden Spoon Charmer**

   (Men Who Marry For Money and the Women Who Let Them)

6. **The Second Chance Ride**

   (When His Wagon is Already Loaded)

7. **The Silver-Haired Fox**

   (When it is a Dead-End Relationship)

OPENING STATEMENT

When, as a woman of destiny, you seek true love for marriage, you will encounter various scenarios with different types of suitors and love interests. These may make or break you; they will either propel you to your destiny or derail you from your destiny completely. You must therefore ensure that any relationship you engage in aligns with your purpose and destiny.

Select your potential suitor without compromise; no matter how handsome, famous, or connected a person is, ask yourself whether he is part of your destiny. Find a suitor who has a revelation and passion about destiny like you do and who knows where he is going. Make sure his dreams resonate with yours. Take time to determine whether you have any shared values, whether you are headed in the same direction, and whether you are on the same page regarding the fundamental issues of life. You must make your destiny your priority when making your choices for true love.

In this section, we will examine the seven common suitors and scenarios that pose as real dilemmas in one's quest not only for true love but for true love that is destiny enhancing. Then, we will summarize those qualities that make a suitable suitor for the purposes of your destiny. Your ability to make a right choice regarding your suitor must be based solely on how much value you place on your destiny and the degree to which you will make sacrifices to put your destiny first. This is the acid test.

In your quest for true love, you will encounter some common suitors that you have heard about from the time you were a teenager. You heard about them either from your mother, your mother's friends, or from your aunts, all of whom may have been victims in their own search for suitors. In those early years of your womanhood, even though you were young, you knew without a shadow of doubt that those kinds of suitors were a "no-go zone." This was not because your mother and aunts told you so, but rather because in your own young heart and mind you could not imagine even in your wildest dreams being caught up with such suitors. Yet, as you grew up and encountered life in all its dynamics and dramas, you found yourself repeating history by daring to consider those exact types of suitors - the very same ones that you were warned about by older and wiser advisors! You did not forget their wisdom or develop amnesia or dementia, but simply because this is how life is.

In this chapter, I am going to encourage you to ask some important questions. Have you sufficiently healed from the pain of your past relationships to the extent that you can confidently and healthily connect with someone in a new relationship? When you have been wounded in past relationships, you can develop a violent resentment of any seemingly happy relationship around you. You can engage in vicious criticism and dismissive cynicism, thereby denying yourself the prospect of a happy relationship for yourself. As the saying goes, any idea that you reject can never benefit you.

Likewise, are you penalizing your current relationship with the offences that were committed against you in your previous relationships? It is entirely possible to sabotage a potentially good relationship because you are still operating in a defensive posture, putting up your guard for fear of being hurt again. Subconsciously, you do not allow yourself to appreciate and trust this new relationship and in your wounded dysfunction you end up pushing him away. You cannot enter a relationship seeking a guarantee against pain and hurt because there is no such indemnity in true love.

Perhaps the one thing that poses the greatest danger to your destiny is your emotions. The toxic power of unhealed pain in your heart has the power to paralyze you, in the process incapacitating you from fulfilling your purpose and destiny. Your choices that impact your destiny will always be distorted and impaired by your anger, bitterness, resentment and unforgiveness. Remember, the victim syndrome always ends up in automatic self-sabotage.

Your solution here is to seek immediate healing because fulfilling your destiny and emotional pain are like oil and water; they can never mix.

It should be noted that the dilemmas raised here are from real life situations that real women have encountered. They have lived to tell the tale to help other women. The advice and solutions offered here are deliberately simple rather than comprehensive and detailed because the intention of this chapter is to highlight the issues and provoke you to ask if you are in any one of these scenarios. That way you can seek professional guidance and support from experts who are qualified and anointed in relationship counselling and marriage guidance. Fortunately, there is no shortage of marriage and relationship experts, coaches, mentors, and counsellors in the marketplace and in the church, so every woman serious about her destiny should take advantage of the available resources. That way you can safeguard your calling and destiny while continuing in the quest for true love and marriage.

Our menfolk may complain that the seven suspect suitors described here are unfair caricatures. To those who argue that men have been unfairly treated, you should know that for each of these male character types there is "a suspect suitress" who mirrors each of the suspect suitors. Know then that each of these relationship dilemmas are caused by both men and women, not just by men. A description of these suspect suitresses is provided at the end of each section.

Let us now look at the critical relationship dilemmas many women testify they have had to grapple with, and from which we can learn valuable lessons.

1. THE WOLF IN SHEEP'S CLOTHING

(When You Have Conflicting Values)

This is a suitor who pretends to be what he is not to get what he wants. This suitor has been all over the place with all types of girls, but he knows that when the time comes to get married, he does not want those he has been with, but he wants an innocent girl. He decides to invade the sectors where such women might be found, as a wolf in sheep's clothing, so that he can entice a "nice one" he believes will make a good wife. He is, of course, misguided because the quality or character of a woman is not necessarily dependent on which sector, she lives in, on whether she is religious, a former girl guide, or whatever. No matter which sector she is in, a woman will make a personal choice based on character or moral uprightness.

This suitor has serious hidden character flaws and behavioural issues; he is certainly not a good boy but hopes to hide who and what he really is until he has put a ring on the woman's finger. Then his "wolf-like nature" will come out. Before that, he sets out to learn all he can about your beliefs and values and he even begins to show interest in what interests you. He learns your lingo and your culture, as well as your goals, dreams, and visions, which he comes to know like the back of his hand. He gets to know your interests, passions, hobbies, and other things you like – such as art, food, music, and so on - and he aligns himself accordingly to give you the impression that the two of you have a lot in common. He seems to be in a hurry to put a ring on your finger because he knows that the longer the courtship goes on and the more time you spend together, the greater the risk that his real self will come out under pressure and stress. *"The devil doesn't come in a red cape and pointy horns; he comes as everything you've ever wished for"* (unknown).

This kind of suitor is a charlatan, an imposter, one who masquerades. As the courtship continues, you notice him cracking under pressure and start to see ugly sides to his personality. You learn things about his questionable character and suspect lifestyle. These things surprise you because they do not align with what he purports to be; they contradict the perfect profile he has presented to you. Your strategy with this kind of suitor is to extend the courtship rather than accelerate it, allowing time for your mature trusted friends to vet and scrutinize him and to give you honest feedback. Don't rush into commitment. If you hold vastly different values and spiritual beliefs now, don't falsely assume that you'll get him to turn around or change his ways later. It may happen, but it may not. Be careful not to settle for less than what you would want for the health and care of your marriage.

Someone once said that *"it is not the wolf who looks like a wolf who is most dangerous. It is the wolf who looks like the sheep."*

The wolf in sheep's clothing has wicked motives; behind every wolf in sheep's clothing is a trail of dead sheep.

The way to recognize a wolf in sheep's clothing is by noting the following factors.

- **Firstly**, wolves (unlike shepherds) only feed themselves and they never feed the sheep. Such a suitor will have selfish tendencies; he puts himself and his own interests first. He does not concern himself with your interest and opinions. So, remember what someone has said, *"People should be judged not by their outward demeanour, but by their works. For many in sheep's clothing do the work of wolves."*
- **Secondly**, a wolf will always snarl whenever he is provoked. Under provocation, his predatorial character comes out because a wolf is the natural enemy of the sheep. A shepherd does not snarl at the sheep but handles them lovingly and patiently.
- **Thirdly**, wolves will play with your emotions, manipulating

you to the point where you trust them, only then to pounce on and devour you. Remember the wise words of caution: "*It is not until the wolf has you hooked that they shed off their sheep's clothing. By then they may have already bitten deeply into your soul.*"

- **Fourthly**, a wolf's story never adds up because it is woven with lies and is full of gaps.
- **Fifthly**, a wolf camouflages its intentions; his motives and agendas towards you are never open and transparent.
- **Sixthly**, a wolf will always have problems submitting to authority. If you have an employer, boss, or spiritual leader to whom you are submitted, this wolf will cunningly plant seeds to make you question your obedience and loyalty to these authority figures.
- **Seventhly**, this wolf suitor will always operate with false information and distorted reports. He will be very economical with the truth.

The scenario associated with this kind of suitor is commonly known as "**The Bird and the Fish Dilemma.**" This arises when there is a conflict of values, beliefs, principles, culture, and socialization.

"A bird and a fish may fall madly in love, but where shall will they live?" **by Elizabeth Gilbert**

Can your relationship survive a conflict in personal values? A bird lives in the air and a fish in the water. For either to compromise would mean certain death. So, you must look beyond the surface and check whether this suitor is suitable. A man is not a dress that you can casually adjust if it doesn't fit, let alone return to the shop and swap for another.

If this kind of dilemma is not resolved, it will have a hugely negative impact on your ability to fulfil your purpose and destiny. Your destiny hinges on your ability to establish and live by certain principles, beliefs, values, and ethics. On these you will base your decisions at every crossroad and at every stage in your journey. Consequently, you cannot afford to be yoked and entangled in a relationship or marriage with someone whose beliefs, principles, values, and ethics differ so fundamentally from yours. Such a partner will derail you from the path of your destiny or cause you to compromise. You can argue that you will be strong enough to be the one to make him change his ways, but this is a very risky thing to assume. If you find yourself in this relationship dilemma, you will need expert advice, especially if you have already made the mistake of entering a committed relationship or even a marriage.

The female version of this **"Wolf in Sheep's Clothing"** is a **"She-Wolf in Ewe's Clothing."** She demonstrates traits similar to the wolf in sheep's clothing; she uses deception and pretence to get what she wants.

The **"She-Wolf in Ewe's Clothing"** has hidden character flaws and serious behavioural issues and is certainly not a good girl. When provoked, her true predatorial character will manifest. A **she-wolf** will only be interested in feeding herself and putting herself first. She has hidden wicked motives towards her suitor. Her stories never add up because they are woven with lies and gaps. She will toy with her suitor's emotions and manipulate him to trust her - until he puts a ring on it, then she unleashes her true colours.

Typically, a **She-Wolf in Ewe's Clothing** will seek to find out everything that her unsuspecting suitor is looking for in a woman, and then she will adopt and wear those traits - for example, being softly spoken, agreeable, very presentable and pleasing, stroking his ego and making him feel like a true hero.

Another version is the woman who becomes a she-wolf out of necessity to survive in the relational jungle of life. She feels that there is no other way to make it through life successfully. This

She-Wolf is not born that way and may have once been among the kindest of women. It took one or more major wounds to make her vicious. Anyone who has dealt with a wounded, bitter, and angry woman knows how much harm she can inflict, especially to men. Such a woman has become a reactionary predator. She needs to be understood and shown compassion, yet that does not mean she will stop being dangerous. Just like a wolf in the wild, she will destroy her prey and devour it should the opportunity arise.

A **She-Wolf** can be found in families as a mother, aunt, sister, daughter, and even a grandmother. She can be married, single, divorced, or widowed. She can be in the corporate world and in the creative arts. If one is married to one or works for one, one can receive much pain and abuse from them.

A **She-Wolf** typically goes after men, especially strong, confident men. Her attacks on these men come in the form of disrespect, talking down at him, mistreatment, downgrading his position. This leaves them feeling emasculated socially and emotionally.

At other times, a **She-Wolf** tends to attract only weak and soft men whom she can totally control and disdain. She wonders why she cannot attract men that will courageously protect and defend her. Emasculated men who have her as a mother or are married to her can easily and secretly hate and resent her. Experienced strong men will see this dangerous creature from afar and will avoid her. She will conclude that the relationship is simply not worth the trouble.

A **She-Wolf** is a wounded woman. At one time or another, she has received mortal wounds from persons she trusted or assumed were safe. Eventually, she chose to stop the bleeding and started to turn the tables to survive the jungle. She was probably wounded by an influential and trusted man or series of men. This could have been her own father, stepfather, grandfather, husband, boyfriend, male friend, or other.

Lopez De Victoria's article 'Beware of She-Wolves' is well worth reading.

2. THE SERIAL DEAL CHASER

(When He Has a Breadwinner Deficiency Syndrome)

Proverbs 13:4 says this: *"The soul of the lazy man desires and has nothing; but the soul of the diligent shall be made rich."*

The **Serial Deal Chaser** is a suitor with dysfunctional money habits and work ethics. This is the man who wants to be taken care of financially. He has no hesitation in being a kept man, nor does he make any apology for it. He is like a beautiful wall hanging; he looks good next to you and enjoys the envy of your friends who "woo" and "ah" at what a handsome hunk you have managed to hook. Little do they know the whole story.

This kind of a man is allergic to paying any bill or expense when you are out together. He pretends to forget his wallet whenever the time comes to pay for something. He does not have any viable means of income or employment. He is constantly pursuing and waiting for a multibillion-dollar deal to come through, but it never seems to happen. This is always a mega deal. He cannot explain why he does not just go for regular, normal-sized deals. There is also an element of pride and self-delusion in him. This makes him presumptuous and unrealistic about his endeavours. As someone has said, *"You cannot have a million-dollar dream with a minimum wage work ethic."*

This **Serial Deal Chaser** does not believe that he should lift a finger or break a sweat in making that transaction come through, nor does he believe in following the proper legal procedures. Instead, he relies on favours in the form of other people's connections and networks (mainly yours, your family's and those of your friends) and he often handles these in a very unprofessional and rude manner, behaving as if they owe him. He operates with a spirit of entitlement and by the time he is through with those connections and networks he will have destroyed all the bridges that took you and your friends and family years to build, and which will equally take you years to rebuild.

In an alternative scenario, you may be a hardworking empowered woman with a high-profile job, a successful mega business, or a powerful public position of influence. If you decide to marry him, you make enough money to cover both of you. The reason you may be reluctant to address this suitor's dysfunctions (bad money habits and lack of work ethics) is because you do not foresee any real financial lack or problem.

This kind of relationship can only last for so long because your financial empowerment will gradually start exposing his inadequacy and his insecurities. Eventually, he will resent you because this arrangement is not natural, and it reflects badly on him. As you continue to rise to greater heights of success, you will start becoming less available, which poses another problem because he starts feeling neglected. To this suitor you represent a provider. You are not, in his estimation, a lover or a potential spouse, with whom there are equally shared responsibilities. If you do marry him, he may eventually seduce someone else to whom he can be a provider and use your money and resources to do so. A **Serial Deal Chaser** is a like a "straw man" partnering with an iron lady. Over time, this kind of man becomes insecure as he feels emasculated. He may even become abusive whether emotionally or physically out of his frustrations. Remember what Pravinee Hurbungs said: *"A strong man can handle a strong woman. A weak man will say she has an attitude."*

It is imperative that at the onset of this kind of relationship you open your eyes and look out for any red flags that could point to your suitor being this kind of man. Avoid men with the chronic bread winner deficiency syndrome where the roles are reversed and the man abdicates his God-given role of provider - where you, the woman, become the main or sole provider instead of the two of you sharing the responsibilities. If you are supporting your boyfriend and paying for everything now – and yet he is healthy and able to work if he wanted to - this may not change afterwards. Always check whether he is a hard-working honest man who is willing and ready to work and apply himself. Perhaps he has encountered a dry, barren season where, despite his every effort, he is unable to lock into a job or a business out of no fault of his own. Perhaps he has previously been a hard-working successful man, but due to circumstances beyond his control, he has lost his job or business and you meet him under those unfortunate circumstances. You obviously cannot write off such a man or judge him unfairly.

If he meets all the other qualifications, then he should be given a chance, especially where you share fundamental values and beliefs and he is a destiny-oriented man. Observe whether he is ready to humble himself for whatever job opportunities that are available. These do not have to be big openings with large salaries. Also, check whether he has any undisciplined spending habits or addictions. These may lead him to accumulate insurmountable debts which will affect you adversely because you will end up paying them yourself under emotional pressure or duress. As Evan Esar says, *"A lazy man's wife is generally the power behind the throne."*

If you make the mistake of marrying a **Serial Deal Chaser** with these habits, then these dysfunctional patterns can only get worse when the stressors of family life and responsibilities begin to mount higher and higher. Remember that money problems and financial struggles are one of the main causes of marital conflicts.

As someone has said, *"A real woman can do it all by herself, but a real man won't let her."*

A **Serial Deal Chaser** will sometimes also portray the traits of a playboy because every time he feels insecure about your empowerment, and every time his conscience pricks him for not taking up his God-ordained role as a provider, he will act as a victim and seek comfort from other less empowered women who he hopes will boost his ego.

Behaviours established before marriage are not going to magically go away once you say, "I do." If it is obvious from the outset that a **Serial Deal Chaser** does not share your values and principles as regards work ethics, principles, and morals, then from the outset the relationship is a non-starter. Where you imagine he loves you enough to make a radical transformation then perhaps it would be best for you to first allow the transformation before you commit yourself to marriage, otherwise your capacity to fulfil your destiny will be greatly hampered or even completely neutralised.

While it is commonly accepted that in today's dispensation where women have become more empowered than they were before, and most are as productive as men in the job market and earning capacity - shared financial responsibilities are now usually the norm. Nonetheless, the man, as the leader and head priest of the family, should take the lead unless prevented by circumstances beyond his control. It is more natural for a man to want to be a bigger provider than his wife and it is not natural for a man to want to be the lesser provider. This is a truth that we find in all cultures.

And what about the female counterpart to this serial deal-chasing man? She is the **"Soap Opera Diva"** - a woman who is allergic to any hard work that will require her to apply herself. She spends her days addicted to soap operas, attending long lunches and high teas, going to the spa with her girlfriends instead of engaging herself in a serious fulltime income-generating job which will require her to be disciplined and productive. She begins one business after another which she never follows through, so she leaves behind her a trail of unfinished issues and clutter. She suffers from an inability to be committed to anything long enough and to that extent it is difficult to take her seriously.

This woman is spoiled. Little girls should not grow up to be spoiled women. There is nothing wrong with liking good things and wanting a man to provide for his family. However, when a woman feels entitled to things without making any contribution, she is not cut out for a successful marriage. To spoil is to change the character of something because of "excessive indulgence" – such as a woman's character which has been compromised because of wealth or material substance. Her ego, anxieties about control, and notions of her marital role regarding finances will bring about major conflicts because she will argue that her role is to be provided for entirely by her spouse.

This kind of woman is lazy. Laziness is often a by-product of being spoiled, but some people are lazy without being spoiled. A solid work ethic is important for a happy marriage. If one or both spouses are not willing to work, marriage will be difficult. A work ethic is not about drawing a pay- check; it's about consistently making the effort required for a successful life. Whether at a job, around the house, or in the relationship, laziness will kill a marriage. If a person is lazy while dating, they will likely be just as lazy in a marriage.

This woman is a parasite. She may end up losing her voice and her power of choice because she compromises her views, beliefs, and principles to align with those of her spouse, to be granted her desires. She may end up being oppressed when she and her spouse differ on some issues, becoming emotionally blackmailed by her spouse, thereby weakening her position in the marriage. She may end up realizing that she is losing herself due to their unstable relationship, which is one-sided because the husband is always in control and dictating how things should run. This is due to his financial muscle as the sole provider. By the time she realizes this, she may not remember who she truly is. Her tendency to depend on him may lead to her losing her husband's respect. She may start resenting him as domineering and authoritarian, yet she is the one who lost her own place, influence, and role as his wife due to her lazy and entitled attitude.

Kevina Thompson's article '**Five Types of Women You Should Marry**' is well worth reading.

3. THE GOLDEN HEIR/THE BEARDED BABY

(When He is a Mama's Boy)

The Golden Heir (aka the Bearded Baby) is usually younger than you. Maybe he has never been married and has no children. He is usually the son of a single mother and is her hope and glory. He is responsible, well-educated, financially and emotionally strong, because his mother has sacrificed to the bone to give him every advantage in life while denying herself even the most basic needs. At this stage, his mother feels she can sit back because she has accomplished her mission and her boy is now making good solid money and can take care of her. She remains hawkeyed, watching out for any girl who dares rock her comfortable boat.

Maybe you are either divorced (so there is the daddy of your baby in the background) or widowed (so you have your late husband's family to contend with) and you may also have your two or three children. You don't want to have any more children, so you are looking for a relationship in which you can begin to find yourself as your children grow, one which allows you to embark on self-development in your career or business.

This **Golden Heir** of course wants kids – or, perhaps it is his mother who cannot imagine him not bringing her grandchildren - but because he is so taken by your maturity, sophistication and strength (he is attracted to women who are as strong as his mother, after all), he begins to believe that maybe he does not need to have his own kids because he can simply step in as a father to your children (to the horror of his mother). This is where his mother will start seeing you as a "Jezebel", which is a very harsh and premature judgment.

This kind of relationship will be rocked by stormy waves such as his mother's resentment, or your baby's father's jealousy about this suitor daring to become a hero and provider to his children (especially where he has fallen short on his duties and responsibilities as a father). Eventually, this suitor may wake up and smell the coffee once he begins to feel short-changed. He may start feeling that the sacrifice is too high and his infatuation with your maturity and strength may begin to diminish. He may even leave you for a "**golden heiress**" to whom he will feel more aligned and less burdened or stressed.

A relationship with this kind of suitor - **The Golden Heir** - may pose challenges because you may both be at different spaces in your life and it would take serious revaluation and realigning for both of you – at the end of a period of expert advice and long-term counselling - to make it workable.

This suitor may also come in a different guise, as someone who had the opportunity to be educated and make something of himself but did not; he is therefore spoilt and entitled and still very dependent on his single mother financially and emotionally. He probably still lives with his mother or he spends so much time with her that he might as well be living with her. This is the **Bearded Baby**.

We all love a man who loves his mama because in our eyes it demonstrates, whether true or false, that he is a man who will always give proper attention to those he loves. Sometimes, however, the boundaries can become blurred. If your suitor still has every bill paid by his mama, and if she controls every decision he makes, he will end up caring more about what mama thinks than what you think. Wake up and smell the coffee because there will be a struggle ahead. A **Bearded Baby** is attracted to older mature women who represents his mother. The chances are he is subconsciously looking for a mother figure to nurture and spoil him. You will not be the only woman in his life; he has an unbreakable bond with his mama. He is her everything and vice versa. There will be three of you in this relationship which is bound to cause a lot of challenges. While two's company, three is a crowd. He will not be independent or his own man and unfortunately, he may end up being his mama's puppet, controlled and manipulated to dance to her tune. He will expect everything to be done for him (by you or his mama), including making decisions. This will drain you physically, mentally, and emotionally, especially since he will not be in a position to be of any support to you.

He will always compare you with his mama, sometimes subconsciously, but you will never live up to his mama's standard and you will not always come first in his life. You will not be his priority and he will always bail out on you to rush and attend to his mama. Unfortunately, his mama may use this to disrupt your relationship to the point where, God forbid, it becomes a lifelong struggle, a competition between you and his mama where you are constantly trying to outsmart one another.

One of the leading causes of divorce is relationship difficulties with mothers-in-law. Even though there is no perfect family, you must make sure you are both on the same page when it comes to leaving, cleaving, and uniting. If there is trouble with drawing healthy boundaries before you are married, there most definitely will be trouble later. Remember the words of Jesus in **Matthew 19:5**: *"For* *this reason a man shall leave his father and mother and be joined to his wife, and the two shall become one flesh."*

This unhealthy mother-son bond may take a miracle to break because the problem is with both people. As a **Bearded Baby**, he may never quite leave and cleave enough to enter a healthy and meaningful relationship with you.

Your ability to fulfil your purpose and destiny while entangled with a **Bearded Baby** and his mama may prove difficult if not impossible. Seek expert advice on whether such a relationship can be worked out and turned around so that you may fulfil your purpose and destiny. A mother- son bond like this, which usually arises where there has been an absentee father (among other factors which experts in this field can expound very well), creates a **Bearded Baby** who has never had any male modelling. This means he may be unable to step into the role of a husband and father as he never saw his father relating to his mother, or his father relating to him. Unless he receives some expert help in overcoming these challenges, he will not relate to you as an equal or as a lover but as his mother.

A **Bearded Baby** will suffer from an identity crisis unless this mother wound is addressed, unless he becomes secure in his identity, then he cannot discover and fulfil his own purpose and destiny. Yoking yourself with such a person will obviously prejudice your ability to fulfil your own purpose and destiny.

The female counterparts to these two male figures are the "**Golden Heiress**" and the "**Daddy's Girl.**"

The **Golden Heiress** is a bit like a **Silver Spoon Girl** in the sense that she has come from a privileged background. She is loaded with an inheritance that she is either already enjoying or waiting to access. When she enters a relationship, she will be the stronger one economically which may lead to various dilemmas. For example, her husband may become insecure if she uses her economic strength to emasculate and lord it over him, whether knowingly or unknowingly. In addition, her economic strength may become a source of conflict between them, especially if her family dangles a carrot to make her conform to what they want in exchange for them releasing her inheritance. She will then have a conflict between submitting to her family or her spouse. Her loyalties will be divided.

As for the **Daddy's Girl**, she may not come loaded with an inheritance or wealth, but she will come loaded with her daddy's influence. She is the apple of her father's eye and her father is her hero. Few men can live up to her expectations; she will constantly compare them to her father. When it comes to her decisions, she will have to choose who to consult, her father or her spouse. Her spouse will constantly live under his shadow.

A **Daddy's Girl** has high self-esteem, self-image, and self-confidence because of the affirmations she received from her dad. How her dad approaches life will serve as the foundation for her own life and set the tone for the kind of man she longs to marry. A dad can therefore create a daughter's conscious and unconscious relationship expectations. If the dad often agreed with his daughter, even when she was wrong, the daughter will expect that her future spouse will always approve of what she does. If the dad set a good example of integrity and honesty, avoiding hypocrisy and admitting his own shortcomings, she will have a realistic and positive example of how to deal with the world, and she will expect the same of her spouse. If her dad modelled a reflective approach to life's big questions, she will seek to do the same and she will expect the same of her spouse.

A woman's early relationship with her dad, who is usually the first male object of her love, shapes her conscious and unconscious perceptions of what she can expect and what is acceptable in a romantic partner.

At the negative end of the same spectrum, a **Daddy's Girl** can become entitled and overly confident and spoilt. She can be highly independent which can cause trouble in a romantic relationship. This may result in conflict especially where she and her husband differ in their opinions on life. If her father was wealthy and gave her all she desired, then her spouse will either need to go beyond her father, meeting her wildest dreams, or, at the very least, match her father in generosity.

4. THE SUPERSTAR a.k.a DRAMA KING

(When You are His Trophy not His True Love)

The **Superstar** aka the **Drama King** is a suitor for whom your physical beauty is an obstacle preventing him from seeing the deeper inward issues necessary in a real relationship. This is not an uncommon problem in relationships. As Aleksandr Serebryakov says, *"People search for love based on appearance, but they forget about attitude and personality."*

The **Drama King** can often be a social celebrity or public figure who loves the limelight. He can be a social media addict who has become hooked on his public image - a sportsman, actor, media personality, politician, or a musician. He is really looking for a trophy to complete his image, a beauty queen to hang on his arm. The surest dealbreakers for him are your beauty and your figure. Steer clear of these men. As someone once said, *"Do yourself a favour by never becoming friends with people who give excessive importance to popularity and social status."*

The **Drama King's** world is centred on your physical appearance and perhaps any minor celebrity status that you may have which, for him, comes as a bonus. Maybe you are a model or a beauty pageant champion. If so, watch out for the trophy hunter; he has no interest in your inner self and he has no experience in meaningful relationships. For him, it's all about outward appearances and public image.

The **Drama King** will keep "polishing" you as if you were a prized trophy because he thrives on what the public thinks of you and him as individuals and as a couple. This means that he will control how you dress, how you do your makeup and hair, and will be horrified at any signs of you putting on weight or appearing unkempt. Anything he perceives as being wrong with you will reflect badly on him, damaging his own image and social status. In this kind of relationship, you are an appendage to his inflated ego. He has forgotten the truth uttered by Mandy Hale that *"outer beauty pleases the eye, but inner beauty captivates the heart."* He is a social climber who plans your lives around events where you can mingle with the "who's who" crowd. He expects you to keep up appearances and adopt every fad that is trending. All this is vanity. As John Ruskin once said, *"The common practice of putting up appearances with society is a mere selfish struggle of the vain with the vain."* If your suitor cares more about what he looks like in the mirror on any given day, if he can't seem to get enough of his awesomeness, and if he is obsessed with your physical beauty and appearance without any interest whatsoever in your inner self, then you may have trouble ahead.

No matter how handsome he is or how beautiful you are, a good marriage is built on deeper foundations than mere outward appearance. As someone has rightly said, *"Appearance captures a woman's attention. Personality captures her heart."*

The **Drama King** may be a bit older than you in age or, if not older in age, he is probably more educated or sophisticated. He seeks to lord it over you because he believes he is better than you and thinks he knows more than you. Basically, he wants to marry a "student" or a "protégé" who he can mould and control for the rest of your lives. To that extent, he is not interested in someone with whom he can partner or make decisions in a synergistic relationship where you value each other's opinions. He will control you, not because he wants to be malicious and cruel but because deep down, he sincerely but erroneously believes that this is the way things are done, maybe because of what he has seen modelled by his parents or his peers. He honestly does not know better, so he believes that he should dictate the way you dress or look, your friendships, your hobbies and activities, your career if any, your business, and vocation. This will include your faith, your church, including how often you should attend.

What seems to be disguised earlier on in the relationship as "I'm only trying to help you," can really be control. This man will dominate and strive to make every decision for you. He will monitor your every move. He will have irrational trust issues, suffocating and oppressing you with his jealousy, possessiveness, and insecurities.

Sometimes, the trophy collector may be very wealthy, living off a pension pot and he entices you with unlimited abundance and a life beyond your dreams. The trap here is everything comes at a price - in this case, your freedom. You lose your voice, independence, drive, and passion for destiny. To him you are a trophy and a possession that he feels he owns for as long as you remain outwardly beautiful. The day you begin to lose the outward beauty that attracted him he will see nothing else of value in you, especially since he never got to know your inward self. He will upgrade to a newer model - one he can mould into his image.

This type of suitor hampers and derails your purpose and destiny because he is obviously more focused on the outward and temporal not on the inward and eternal, and he already has a problem with his self-identity which means he has a problem being destiny-oriented. His control will lead to him suffocating and stifling your voice, individuality, authenticity, and self-identity. He will open the door to an identity crisis where your will no longer be able to determine where he ends and where you begin.

Someone once said, *"the need to keep up appearances is a key indicator that something might be wrong on the inside of your life."* His obsession with your outward beauty may push you to adopt unhealthy measures to keep looking like a beauty queen – measures such as plastic surgery and extreme dieting. Keeping up appearances is expensive and can lead to an accumulation of debts. The pressure he will put you under may lead you to engage in stress-relieving habits like substance abuse. The obsession with appearances, public opinion and social status will push you to sacrifice valuable relationships and friendships just because they don't fit the bill and don't conform to the "right image." As someone has pointed out, *"People who are attracted to you because of your pretty face or nice body won't be by your side forever but people who can see how beautiful your heart is will never leave you."*

The female version or mirror image of this Drama King Suitor is "The Slay Queen." There is a new breed of woman in town known on social media as the Slay Queen. **The Slay Queen** is a woman who wants to choke everyone else by telling them how beautiful she feels she is. She over-focuses on her outward looks and appearance. She is inconsistent in her outlook on life. She tells you that a gentleman must match his shoes and belt, yet the colour of her face and neck don't match. That's **The Slay Queen.**

The Slay Queen engages in romantic relationships according to the outward appearance of the man rather than for love. She looks for the most popular man in town, the man with a swag, the man who cares about image as well. **Slay Queens** entice men - especially public figures - because of their looks. They go for breast enhancement surgeries. They bleach their skin if they have a dark complexion. They buy lavish clothes and accessories. This kind of woman will put a lot of pressure on her husband to fund her expensive shopping sprees and to sponsor her extravagant tastes.

5.   THE SILVER AND GOLDEN SPOON CHARMER

(Men Who Marry for Money and the Women Who Let Them)

It has been rightly said that "*those that marry for money lose their liberty.*" The Silver and Golden Spoon Charmer is the suitor who has done his due diligence into your background. He is looking for a situation in which he can access wealth easily and become an overnight success by virtue of riding on your family without any hard labour on his part.

The Silver and Golden Spoon Charmer, quickly makes friends with your family and friends by portraying himself as very presentable and dependable. He endears himself to them as the perfect future son-in-law. This man sets out to marry into money because he does not want the stress of hard work to generate his own income and to create his own wealth. He wants the easy way out and you are his shortcut. He wants to travel through life without paying and you are his golden ticket. You are not his destination; you are just a means to an end. Once he reaches his goal, he will drop you like a hot cross bun.

This suitor does not bother to know you but focuses on knowing about you - your family resources and, most importantly, your ability to access those resources for him because of the favour and trust you have with your family. If he realizes that your sister has more favour with your family than you do, then he has no problem shifting alliances.

This man does his calculations precisely to know your net worth - your inheritance and entitlement. He knows that how he treats you will determine his entry into the "gold reserve" because he understands what a treasure you are to your family.

Initially, he treats you like the princess that you are, and he patiently puts up with all your dysfunctions, idiosyncrasies, proclivities, even when inwardly he is writhing with irritation. He presents himself as a successful well-to-do "consultant", fabricating an impressive but fake profile which is shrouded with mystery and many unanswered questions which he covers up as confidential information – which you and your family fall for.

He is the epitome of respect, politeness, knowledge, is extremely well read and even well educated, portraying the image that he knows will impress you and your family. In fact, one might call him brilliant which is why it is so sad when he chooses to use all his intelligence deceiving others instead of creating his own wealth. He is a prime example of a man using a good mind for bad purposes.

Then he starts on his life goals!

This suitor speaks of his mega investment plans, name dropping to imply that he has joined all the appropriate social clubs and cliques because he knows what will give him credibility. All the while he is under a weight of debt. One of the red flags you should see if you are alert – and if you want to see - is the fact that he appears more interested in impressing and spending time with your family than with you. This is because he has a well calculated strategy to get your family on his side which he knows will pressure you into committing to him, even when you may have a nagging feeling which you can't put your finger on that something isn't quite right and all may not be well.

He is a smooth talker, persuasive, with a very subtle controlling spirit which he camouflages as wisdom. This kind of a suitor usually aims to become the "king's son-in-law" so that he can gains access to the throne and the vault, giving him the chance to be sorted for life. He is very aware that nothing will come to him without you because you are the "bait" or the "worm" he is trying to use to haul in the catch. You must be wise and undertake your own fishing expedition by engaging him in subtle conversations to test his motives. Be sharp enough to do your own due diligence, scrutinizing his friendships and networks, because for sure you will find something that gives the game away.

In this scenario above this suitor targets **The Silver Spoon Babe** who was born into a wealthy family of high social standing with wealth waiting for her to inherit. No one judges her for the fact that she didn't have to work for it and it is given to her unconditionally. **Silver spoon babes** sometimes grow up spoilt and feeling entitled and never acquired discipline, hard work, and ethics. They may end up losing or wasting their inheritance in the long run for lack of character and good life choices.

This **Silver Spoon Babe** is also referred to as a **Trust Fund Baby** or a **Golden Heiress** and she often becomes a prime target for the **Silver Spoon Charmer**. Although she may see red flags, she will still end up with this suitor, wasting her money and resources on him, even though there is no true love and no real commitment.

In another scenario, the charmer may target "**The Golden Spoon Lady**" - the woman who is more mature than the Silver Spoon Babe; she was not born into wealth or status but with values and principles that were instilled in her like discipline, hard work, excellence, diligence, persistence, integrity, and sacrifice. These enabled her to create her own wealth over time and to succeed in gaining status, credibility, and even powerful positions of influence.

This **Golden Spoon Lady** is mature, well-established, empowered, intelligent and wise. Perhaps she is divorced, widowed or a single woman or single mother. This suitor is therefore likely to be younger than her. He is a man who preys on this type of woman so that he can live off her. He knows that she is financially stable and that she is not looking for a rich man but simply a man who will love her and make her feel attractive again. She may grasp at this opportunity as another chance for happiness.

This Golden Spoon lady calculates this relationship and concludes that she can handle it because:

- She believes herself too mature and wise to make the same mistakes as she did when she was younger in her relationships with men
- She believes that since this suitor is younger than her, he is presumably also not as wise as her, so she will be able rein him in without any risks (especially where in her previous relationships she was the one who was controlled and oppressed)
- She believes she is at an age and in a place in her life where she deserves to spoil herself, to have some adventure and stop being so uptight
- She believes that she is too secure in her self-identity to be controlled by anyone so she believes that she is the one who is going to "play" the charmer
- She believes that since he has presented himself as one who is doing well financially (although this turns out to be a misrepresentation) then it means that he doesn't need to encroach on her wealth and resources.

Unfortunately, this suitor has already conducted his research into this lady, so he already knows how she thinks. By the time she falls in love with him, her strategy comes tumbling down like the house of cards that it is (because she underestimated his deceptive charm and she failed to calculate that she may fall in love). This is exactly what he wanted. Now he can reveal his true colours and his true intentions and start manipulating her for her money.

The female version and mirror of this **Silver and Golden Spoon Charmer** is the "**Golden Pension Pot Chaser**." This is the woman who believes that the only way that she can actualize her dreams is by entering a relationship with a man who is already loaded. This will mean that she does not need to stretch or apply herself to make her own wealth.

The **Golden Pension Pot Chaser** will usually target an older, very wealthy man who is looking for an extremely beautiful and attractive woman on whom to lavish his wealth, just so long as she helps to keep him feel young. Depending on the age of the man - usually over 60-years-old - this woman may not necessarily be that young, but she will certainly be much younger than him.

She differs from the college intern girl (the Foxy Vixen) in that she has been around and has quite a bit of experience with relationships. This enables her to be a real charmer. She is crystal clear why she is in this relationship. She is very aware that she may end up playing nurse and caregiver to this man but she has already calculated that this is a price worth paying since she is already living in a lifestyle that is beyond her wildest dreams and she is assured that she stands to inherit a huge fortune.

The **Golden Pension Pot Chaser's** husband is a wealthy pensioner. He is extremely generous. In his mind, the amount he is spending on this woman is a drop in the ocean. He has probably been divorced several times before and is often estranged from his children. He probably had no time for them when they were growing up and there is a lot of resentment in their hearts. He may choose to punish them for their justified anger by not including them in his will.

This means more is left for his young wife. After his death, she will obviously face legal battles from his children and their mother(s), where she may end up a loser.

6. THE SECOND CHANCE RIDE

(When His Wagon is Already Loaded)

This is the suitor who is either divorced or widowed with children. He comes laden with precious and delicate "baggage" or "baby mama drama." He brings with him his ex-wife's menacing shadow or his late wife's daunting memory. He also brings in tow the in-laws, either the menacing type or the daunting type. He brings his children who constantly and unfairly make him feel guilty because of the absence of their mother. In addition, there is his ex-wife's or late wife's friends, as well as his own boys club.

In this scenario, you are either a single woman and have never been married before, with or without children, or you may have been married and you are either now divorced or widowed and you have children or you don't have children.

To that extent, you also come laden with some baggage of your own, whether it be your children, "baby daddy drama", or the weight of your past relationships that left you wounded and disappointed, with a fear of commitment and of ending up in another broken relationship.

This **second chance rider**, type of suitor is **firstly** probably looking for a caretaker for him and his children. He targets the woman who looks like a potential homemaker and nurturer - one who appears selfless, who will easily sacrifice her own interests to put his interests and those of his children first.

Secondly, he may also not be financially stable, so he is probably also looking for a woman's material support and financial means who is willing to bare his burdens.

Thirdly, he obviously does not want more children, so if you are single without children, he will target you as someone he assumes has given up on the idea of having children of her own. He may be wrong; you may want children of your own, even if it's just one, to "tighten the bond" between you. If that is the case, then a dilemma arises immediately because of the conflicting interests and needs between you.

As a single woman with or without children, you must count the cost before you commit to such a man. You need to decide what compromises and sacrifices you are willing to make and which of your interests, goals and dreams you are ready to surrender, or at any rate put on the backburner while you sort out and manage all this precious and delicate baggage.

This kind of relationship is challenging because the suitor may become emotionally unavailable for you because of all his baggage and the demand for his attention, time, and energy. The question is whether there will be enough room for you in his loaded wagon. He would need to be a very mature and consummate organizer to balance all this and still give you the attention and support you need. This would be exasperated if you also bring into the mix baggage that makes you similarly unavailable for him emotionally.

Since children, whether yours or his, are the most delicate part of the scenario, the other pertinent question is whether you are both ready or equipped to parent each other's children, especially if they are teens and young adults, and whether you can accommodate their resentment and constant attempts to dislodge you (which often happens at the beginning). Tales of stepchildren creating a nightmare are not uncommon when both people are torn and where conflict arises between your spouse and your children in a crisis. Sometimes, children work in cahoots with your former spouse, or with the family members of your former spouse, to make it quite clear that there is not enough room for you in the loaded wagon. Do you have the skills and the coping mechanisms for this kind of scenario? Boundaries should be set to preview the roles and mandates clearly, but this is easier said than done.

The other challenge which is often overlooked - because it is not a comfortable issue to deal with when a relationship is in its early stages - is money. This can later become a serious bone of contention. Both his and your material substance - your properties and assets acquired previously should be addressed early in the relationship before you commit to marriage, especially where you both have your own children who you both want to bequeath those properties and assets to. Burying your heads in the sand on money issues can cause untold sorrow and it can come to haunt and ruin your relationship later.

Be honest enough to seek advice and wise counsel from relevant professionals and experts in good faith because the foundation of any relationship that has any chance of survival and success is openness and trust.

Another dynamic of this "**Second Chance Ride**" kind of relationship is where this suitor is still married or living with another woman or women, whether as wives or otherwise, and he is inviting you to enter his "**polygamy potpourri**." He expects you to become a side plan or a side dish that he openly introduces to his other wife or wives and family. In this scenario, bizarrely nobody has a problem with it.

The question is whether you can survive in this potpourri and what sacrifices will you need to make to fit in. Is this what you had bargained for? Are you not settling for less than you deserve?

Many of today's modern women in the marketplace may well argue that times have changed and that binding yourself in a polygamous potpourri is not only practical but also advisable, in view of the current ratio and statistics that for every man there are at least three women. For the woman serious about her destiny, there is an added bind; it's not just about the availability of suitors but is also about the availability of "suitable suitors." Suffice to say that as a woman serious about her destiny, this relationship may pose serious problems because you need to ask yourself crucial questions. If you were to stubbornly and irrationally argue that this polygamous husband is one of your destiny helpers, can you say the same about your co-wives? Are they also your destiny helpers? Or, are they destiny killers?

Anyone you yoke yourself with is either an asset or a liability to your destiny.

Your solution here is to distance yourself completely from this polygamous potpourri because your destiny comes first. You must settle in your heart and spirit that there is either a spouse still out there for you or, if not, God in His wisdom will give you peace to fulfil your destiny and live a happy and fulfilled life without a spouse. Whether it be the loaded wagon or the polygamous potpourri, you should question any relationship that will compromise your ability to fulfil your Calling and Destiny.

The female version of this suitor is the "**Mama Cinderella**." At one extreme, she is a woman divorced or widowed and loaded with delicate baggage, so her agonies and dilemmas compare with the man who is the **Second Chance Rider**. However, since men and women perceive things differently in a relationship, it is possible that this woman will be able to handle this same scenario much better than the man. By the time a woman has decided to get herself into such a relationship, she will have thought long and hard. She will have analyzed every angle and come up with strategies how not only to survive but also to thrive. She will have considered how to make it work, provided the man and his children cooperate with her. She will have mastered the art of tiptoeing and sidestepping around any landmines to minimize any tensions and conflict.

At the other extreme is the woman who has never been married before and has no children. She has no baggage and will face totally different dilemmas and challenges, depending on whether she is young or a middle-aged.

The younger version of this woman may want her own children and she may not be strong and experienced enough to raise her spouse's children. In addition, she may not get the undivided attention she needs from her spouse, who already has enough people to whom he needs to give his attention.

As for the middle-aged, more mature woman (who has also never been married and doesn't have children), she may not want to have children, so the only question is whether she is willing to raise her spouse's children. Her ability to do so may depend on the age of the stepchildren and their attitude towards her. This is essentially a "blended family". **The Mama Cinderella** may experience hardship because of the baggage from both families. If the two families take time to blend, she may be faced with major challenges. For example, sibling rivalry may be a major issue in a blended family. When everyone needs attention, failure to apportion it equally will lead to conflict. Also, a step parent having to discipline a child may be a challenge if the stepchildren resist efforts to keep them in hand.

The stress of conflict over money and resources constitutes one of the most often-cited problems that many who remarry face. **Mama Cinderella** may end up experiencing financial stress where she not only has to deal with her own children but also with those of her spouse. Financial stress can lead to more general stress - more conflict over things unrelated to money, as well as money-centred arguments. Taking care of children requires more responsibility as well as a change in roles. It provides more stress and reduces the amount of time available to bond as a remarried couple. Balancing between her children and her spouse's children may require a lot of sacrifice especially on her side, depending on the age of her spouse's children. Handling discipline and implementing family standards may be a challenge. If she happens to favour her own children over those of her spouse, family harmony may be even more compromised.

Depending on the man's relationship with his ex-wife, **Mama Cinderella** may encounter problems if the former wife tries constantly to sabotage her. She can't view her simply as his "ex" because she is the mother of his children. Any mother is bound to have insecurities about another woman coming into her children's lives. Rome wasn't built in a day, and neither was a family. It will take time to find a rhythm.

This kind of relationship can be a rollercoaster ride. One day the kids seem to like her, and the next they are standoffish. One day things with the ex are going smoothly, and the next, they feel rocky.

In short you need to count the cost before you commit to a **Second Chance Rider.**

Lisa Steinke's article, '**Divorce Dad's Tips for Dating a Divorced Father**,' is well worth reading.

7. THE SILVER HAIRED FOX

(When it is a Dead-End Relationship)

It is clearly a dead-end relationship when a suitor is more than twice your age, most likely a wealthy high-flier. You are still at the "intern" stage in your life; you have just finished studying and have not yet locked into a proper job or career. Perhaps you are doing a temporary job. He entices and impresses you with perfumes, jewellery, chocolate which he brings you from his worldwide travels. These gifts may get upgraded to cars or an apartment, but they are still just enticements and he can take them away anytime. He opens a door to a sophisticated, wealthy lifestyle for which you have not worked, giving you a skewed perspective of life.

This man is often married and has no intentions of leaving his family, so you are just a bright shinny object or a temporary distraction (which could run to ten or more years if you're not careful) to cure the boredom he feels in his family life. You are also a boost to his ego. Such a relationship wastes your time and locks you out of potential genuine relationships at a prime stage of your life. This suitor is merely a loaded tap and you are a thirsty sponge. Eventually, he will leave you and you will be at best "damaged goods", unable to appreciate any relationship with mates or peers of your own age because of the perks and luxuries you had become used to, which a suitor your age cannot afford to give you.

A **Silver Haired Fox** steals valuable seasons and years out of your destiny by derailing your focus, energy, and time. He is not one of your ordained destiny helpers; in fact, he is more like a subtle destiny killer. At the very least, he is a destiny delayer, though you may not see that until the fantasy is over. Sometimes, the regret and pain you feel at how you have been deceived may hold you captive for years, hindering you from fulfilling your call and destiny. The fact that he has no intention of making you a long-term part of his life means that the only impact he can have on your destiny is a negative one – one in which you're left bruised.

This type of suitor deceives you by giving you false hopes that one day he will leave his family and marry you. Remember, he is a *fox*; foxes are cunning. Sometimes a **Silver-haired fox** starts off as a mentor, a genuine sponsor to you, or someone who has seen your potential and sincerely seeks to help and propel you upwards in your career or business ventures by opening the right doors and connecting you with the right people. In essence, he could start off as a destiny helper but due to your innocence, naivety or a desire for the finer things in life, and his irresponsibility and feelings of entitlement (on the grounds that he has helped you), the relationship takes an ugly turn.

The boundaries of decency between you eventually become blurred and crossed, leading to gross moral failure on both your parts. It could be that you feel so grateful and that you owe him, or you feel pressured and under duress to accommodate his inappropriate advances for the sake of your success. It could also be that he strikes when he knows you really need his help and so he more or less uses emotional blackmail to coerce you into a type of relationship that you know is wrong but you feel you have no choice but to accept.

It could even be that you bore a child with him (to his great horror because a child was not a part of his plan). You may be tempted to use that innocent child to destroy his marriage and family. Beware of seeking revenge in that manner. His family may conspire and collude to turn you into the enemy, branding you as a home breaker and marriage wrecker as they move on with their lives. This suitor might be privileged, have a lot of influence and be a law unto himself because everyone around him depends on him financially. None of them therefore has the boldness to question him. His family and those around him have enabled him, normalizing and legitimizing his licentious lifestyle. Chances are you are not the only woman but one among many who have become trapped in the web of his deceit.

The effect of discovering that you were never special to him can erode your self-confidence and self-esteem and thrust you into an identity crisis. You must refuse to allow your error of judgment and your moral failure to hinder or abort your purpose and destiny. Instead, you should own and take responsibility for your mistake and start afresh by making better choices. The fact that you are still young means that there is plenty of time for you to forgive yourself, redeem your past and move on to a very bright future where you will fulfil your calling and destiny, using your past only as a life lesson to caution other young women against the wiles of the **Silver Haired Fox.**

Your other solution is to flee and disconnect yourself from this dead-end relationship and embark on redeeming your missed seasons. If you are faithful, diligent and sincerely remorseful, making a radical turnaround, then there will be a quick work in your life whereby your missed and lost seasons will be restored and you will go on to fulfil your calling and destiny. Your relationship with a **Silver Haired Fox** ultimately interferes with the destiny of other people his wife, his children (who are probably your age), your child with him (if any), your own parents and siblings. Our wrong choices have ugly consequences for us and those we love, but similarly our choice to change will always bless us and bless those we love.

The female counterpart here is the **"Foxy Vixen."** This is a woman who is much younger than the man and is probably still in college or university, or still an intern who wants a special kind of lifestyle overnight. She is not willing to follow the usual processes and wait out the several years it will take for her to earn and afford this kind of lifestyle for herself, so she looks for and settles for an older wealthier man who will lavish her with all the material substance she desires, even though she knows that she is just a plaything and that they are using each other for their own reasons.

This woman is often known as a **Gold Digger**. Don't be deceived. Just because she is young doesn't mean that she isn't seductive. She is glamorous and entitled, manipulative and cunning; she knows what she wants and who to target. She aspires to be classy and works hard at it, often appearing much older and sophisticated than her peers.

This girl is smart. Unlike the Slay Queen, who uses only her looks, a **Foxy Vixen** uses her brains and her ability to manipulate her man. She selects her mate because of the size of his wallet. She figures, who needs chemistry when you can have cash? She will not necessarily keep her man because she loves him. She will use him like she uses a credit card. She accesses its resources when she wants to, the rest of the time it's nothing more than a piece of plastic. In other words, she is a user. She will identify her mate's weakness and exploit it for her own benefit. She is a charmer in the eyes of her lover, and her lover will do everything to protect her, because she behaves like a damsel in distress.

In a more extreme scenario, this **Foxy Vixen** may also marry a man for a few months or years then divorce him just to receive her settlement. In some countries, this is half the estate. She will have planned this even before she met him.

Gold Diggers are women who seek wealthy partners so that they can create the lifestyle they have envisioned for themselves. They are lazy and don't want to work hard for their living. They love to be classy in the way they dress and what they eat. They must have the latest smartphones and drive a desirable car. Their dream is to live in the posh parts of town, all at her man's expense, of course.

This **Foxy Vixen** may never fulfil her Calling and Destiny unless she makes a radical paradigm shift on time.

Conclusion

As a wise woman who does not want to jeopardize her destiny because of dysfunctional love ties, you will need to be cautious in sieving your suitors. Consider the following critical points:

a) Is it possible for you to be "**alone but not lonely**"? Are you running away from yourself? You must learn to have a healthy relationship with yourself first before seeking to commit yourself to a spouse.

b) Keep asking yourself, **are you single by choice or by default**? It is not mandatory for every woman to get married, so resist any pressure if you have already decided to stay single by choice.

c) Have sufficiently healed from your past relationships to enable you to confidently connect to your future relationships?

d) Are you penalizing your current relationships with offences that were committed against you in your previous relationships?

e) What makes you see the warning flags as pink instead of red? What blurs your vision when the signs are so clear?

f) Do your girlfriends own your relationships? Do you feel pressured by your spice girls to make love choices which deep down you know are wrong?

g) Is s prenuptial agreement prudent or a passion killer?

h) When the scales of conflict tip, is he strong enough to protect you from his family? When your in-laws become bylaws can your relationship survive?

i) Why do statistics show that second and subsequent marriages have a higher percentage of failure than first marriages? Does experience not translate to competence? Is it possible that your tolerance decreases over time?

j) Could it be that your inability to lay hold of a happy relationship is due to your violent resentment and cold cynicism of any seemingly happy relationship around you? As the saying goes, "the thing you disrespect and despise can never benefit you."

k) Are your shoes soft enough to tiptoe around the stepchildren? How equipped are you to parent your spouse's children?
l) Can you "zip your own dress", are you able to survive and thrive even without a spouse?

Destiny Questions to Ponder

1. Have you ever been entrapped by **a wolf in sheep's clothing?** What finally made you see through the wool?

2. Is it possible for a serial deal chaser to be reformed?

3. What would be your greatest fear with **a golden heir** or **a bearded baby?**

4. Do you think that **a drama king** can ever change? If so, how?

5. How should a silver spoon babe protect her interests and still find love? What causes an intelligent, empowered, **golden spoon lady to fall** for the deceptive enticements of a **golden spoon charmer?**

6. What would be your greatest fear in a **second chance ride** situation?

7. How would you advice young Women to guard against a **Silver Haired Fox?**

WORDS HAVE POWER

Relevant Quotes and Scripture Meditations

for Your Naming and Defining

Inspirational Quotes and Scriptures about the Woman of Destiny

"Strong women not only feel pain, they accept it, they learn from it and fight through it. They turn their wounds into wisdom. They may fall, but they always get back up, dust off, and fight like they have never fought before." By **Unknown**

"A woman who is at rest with herself has nothing to prove to others, she embraces her strengths & cheers others on with a pure heart. Her light shines brightly; her words are seasoned with kindness, goodness & grace. She is peaceful & edifies others as she is secure in her Heavenly Father." By **Hanna Bryant**

"God has a purpose for your pain, a reason for your struggle and a reward for your faithfulness. Trust Him and don't give." By **Dave Willis**

"She may be quiet, but she's a warrior and her prayers can move mountains." **Unknown**

"She is not broken anymore, she is stronger, wiser and more beautiful than before, because God took her broken pieces and made her new again." By **Unknown**

"Though my soul may set in darkness, it will rise in perfect light; I have loved the stars too fondly to be fearful of the night." By **Sarah Williams**

"In the end, she became more than she was expected. She became the journey, and like all journeys, she did not end, she just simply changed directions and kept going." By **R.M. Drake**

"Mirror! Mirror! on the wall, I'll always get up after I fall. And whether I run, walk or have to crawl, I'll set my goals and achieve them all." By **Brie Edison**

"I am a strong woman because a strong woman raised me." By **Unknown**

"We all have an unsuspected reserve of strength inside that emerges when life puts us to test." By **Isabel Allende**

"Keep your head up. God gives his hardest battles to his strongest soldiers." By **Unknown**

"If you feel like you are losing everything, remember that trees lose their leaves every year and they still stand tall and wait for better days to come." By **Unknown**

"Strength grows in the moments when you think you can't go on, but you keep going anyway." By **Unknown**

"Some women are lost in the fire. Some women are built from it." By **Michelle K**

"I know you're tired, you're fed up, you're so close to breaking, but there is strength within you even when you feel weak. Keep fighting. By **Unknown**

"Strength doesn't come from what you can do. It comes from overcoming the things you once thought you couldn't. By **Rikki Rogers**

"It's actually pretty simple. Either you do it, or you don't." By **Unknown**

"She believed she could, so she did." By **R.S. Grey**

"I'm proud of the woman I am because I went through one hell of a time becoming her." By **Unknown**

"The circles of women in our lives weave invisible nets of love that carry us when we are weak, and they sing with us when we are strong." By **Sark**

"Behind every successful woman is a tribe of other successful women, who have her back." By **Kimberly**

"Women should empower each other, instead of being so hateful and envious of one another." By **Unknown**

"A successful woman is one who can build a firm foundation with the bricks others have thrown to her." By **Unknown**

"It took me quite a long time to develop a voice, and now that I have it I am not going to be silent." By **Madeleine Albright**

"She overcomes everything that was meant to destroy her." By **Sylvester McNutt III**

"When women support each other, incredible things happen." By **Viola Davis**

"Each time a woman stands up for herself, she stands up for all women." By **Maya Angelou**

"A woman is unstoppable after she realizes she deserves better." By **Yene D.**

"I am obsessed with seeing women encourage, support, and empower other women. It's my favorite, we need more of it." By **Unknown**

"I would like to be known as an intelligent woman, a courageous woman, a loving woman, a woman who teaches by being." By **Maya Angelou**

"Here's to strong women, may we know them, may we be them, may we raise them." By **Unknown**

"She never seemed shattered; to me she was the breath-taking mosaic of the battles she won." By **Unknown**

"A strong woman, looks a challenge in the eye, and gives it a wink." By **Gina Carey**

"Never underestimate the power of a kind woman. Kindness is a choice that comes from incredible strength." By **Unknown**

"She surrounds herself with women she can grow with." By **Unknown**

"When a woman is loved correctly, she becomes ten times, the woman she was before." By **Unknown**

"A woman unaffected by insult has made her enemies absolutely powerless." By **Entity**

"A strong woman in her essence is a gift to the world." By **Unknown**

"I want every girl to know that her voice can change the world." By **Malala Yousafzai**

"Women who compliment other women genuinely are a whole different breed. Real Queens" By **Unknown**

"Nothing is more impressive than a woman who is secure in the unique way God made her." By **Rhonda Kulczyk**

"Empowered women empower women." By **Unknown**

"A foolish woman keeps talking, a wise woman understands the power of her words as well as her silence." By **Unknown**

"And one day she discovered, that she was fierce, and strong, and full of fire, and that not even she could hold herself back, because her passion burned brighter than her fears." By **Mark Anthony**

"We need women who are so strong, they can be gentle, so educated they can be humble, so fierce they can be compassionate, so passionate they can be rational, and so disciplined they can be free." By **Kavita N. Ramdas**

"A strong woman is a woman determined to do something others are determined not to be done." By **Marge Piercy**

"Be strong enough to let go, and wise enough to wait for what you deserve." By **Unknown**

"Strong women lift each other up." By **Unknown**

"A woman is like a tea bag; you never know how strong it is until it is in hot water." By **Eleanor Roosevelt**

"A strong woman is one, who feels deeply and loves fiercely, her tears flow just as abundantly as her laughter. A strong woman is both soft and powerful, she is both practical and spiritual, a strong woman in her essence is a gift to the world." By **Unknown**

"Strong women wear their pain like stilettos, no matter how much it hurts, all you see is the beauty of it. By **Harriet Morgan**

"Success isn't about how much money you make, it's about the difference you make in people's lives." By **Michelle Obama**

"To attract money, you must focus on wealth. It is impossible, to bring more money into your life, when you are noticing you don't have enough because that means you are thinking thoughts that you don't have enough." By **Rhonda Byrne**

"You can only become truly accomplished at something you love. Don't make money your goal. Instead pursue the things you love doing and then do them so well that people can't take their eyes off you." By **Maya Angelou**

"Here's to financially independent Women, may we know them, may we be them, may we raise them." By **Unknown**

"People, who have drawn wealth into their lives, used the secret consciously or unconsciously, they think thoughts of abundance of

wealth, and they don't allow any contradictory to take roots in their minds." By **Rhonda Byrne**

"Save your money and one day your money will save you." By **Unknown**

"Nearly every glamorous, wealthy, successful career woman, you might envy now, started out as some kind of schlep. By **Helen Gurley Brown**

"A business career for a woman, and her needs for a woman's life, as wife and mother, are not enemies at all, unless we make them so. But maybe the closest and most co-operative friends and supporters of each other." By **Hortense Oldum**

"Leadership is about making others better as a result of your presence and making sure that impact lasts in your absence." By **Sheryl Sandberg**

"Women need to shift from thinking I'm not ready to do that to I'll learn by doing it." By **Sheryl Sandberg**

"If your actions create a legacy that inspires others to dream more, learn more, do more and become more, then, you are an excellent leader." By **Dolly Parton**

"I just want women to always feel in control, because we are capable, we're so capable." By **Nicki Minaj**

"A leader takes people where they want to go. A great leader takes people where they don't necessarily want to go, but ought to be." By **Rosalynn Carter**

"Because I am a woman, I must make unusual effort to succeed. If I fail, no one will say, 'She doesn't have what it takes.' They will say, women don't have what it takes." By **Unknown**

"Our deepest fear is not that we are inadequate. Our deepest fear is that we are powerful beyond measure." By **Marianne Williamson**

"Leadership is hard to define and good leadership even harder. But if you can get people to follow you to the end of the earth, you are a great leader." By **Indra Nooyi**

"People respond well to those that are sure of what they want." By **Anna Wintour**

"No power on earth compares to a mother's tender prayer." By **Edwin Arnold**

"I remember my mother's prayer and they have always followed me. They have clung to me all my life." By **Abraham Lincoln**

"The battle for our children's lives is waged on our knees." By **Stormie Omartian**

"Prayer warrior mothers cover their kids with God's blessings and protection." By **Marla Alupoaicei**

"Every mother's prayer; guide her to a place where she'll be safe." By **Carole Bayer Sager**

"The bond between mothers and their children is one defined by love. As a mother's prayer for her children are unending, so are the wisdom, grace and strength they provide for their children." By **President George W. Bush**

"God does hear and answer prayers… From childhood, at my mother's knee where I first learned to pray … I know without question that it is possible for men and women to reach out in humility and prayer and tap that Unseen Power." ~**Ezra Taft Benson**

"During all those years of struggle and heartache, my mother never worried. She took all her troubles to God in prayer." ~**Dale Carnegie**

"My mother knew when to listen and when to pray and when to help. I wonder how many people knew the compassion [my mother] held for them and how hard, in the privacy of her God Box, she prayed for them and their struggles." ~**Mary Lou Quinlan**

"To this day, even though I am grown and have two children of my own, whenever I travel somewhere distant or am undertaking a major project, my mother will sit me down, lay hands on me, and say a prayer of blessing." ~**Francisco J. García** Jr.

"From the time of my earliest memories, she impressed upon me one rule above all others: when I woke from sleep, my first duty was to pray to God for spiritual nourishment and blessings . . . my mother would never relent . . . She planted in me, and tended in my early life, a profound love and fear of God." ~**Sadhu Sundar Singh**

Bible Wisdom About The Woman Of Destiny

Proverbs 31:30; "Charm is deceitful and beauty is passing, But a woman who fears the LORD, she shall be praised."

Psalm 46:5 "God is in the midst of her, she shall not be moved; God shall help her, just at the break of dawn."

Proverbs 31:16-17 "She considers a field and buys it; from her profits she plants a vineyard. She girds herself with strength, and strengthens her arms."

1 Corinthians 15:10 "But by the grace of God I am what I am, and His grace toward me was not in vain; but I labored more abundantly than they all, yet not I, but the grace of God *which was* with me."

Proverbs 31:20-21 "She extends her hand to the poor, Yes, she reaches out her hands to the needy. She is not afraid of snow for her household, For all her household *is* clothed with scarlet."

Psalm 139:14 "I will praise You, for I am fearfully and wonderfully made; Marvellous are Your works, And that my soul knows very well."

1 Corinthians 11:12 "For as woman came from man, even so man also comes through woman; but all things are from God."

1 Peter 3:3-4 "Do not let your adornment be merely outward—arranging the hair, wearing gold, or putting on fine apparel—rather let it be the hidden person of the heart, with the incorruptible beauty of a gentle and quiet spirit, which is very precious in the sight of God."

1 Timothy 3:11 "Likewise, their wives must be reverent, not slanderers, temperate, faithful in all things."

Luke 1:45 "Blessed is she who believed that there will be a fulfilment of those things which were told her from the Lord."

Proverbs.31:20 "She extends her hand to the poor, Yes, she reaches out her hands to the needy."

Proverbs 11:16 "A gracious woman retains honor, But ruthless *men* retain riches."

Proverbs 31:25 "Strength and honor *are* her clothing; She shall rejoice in time to come."

Proverbs 3:15 "She *is* more precious than rubies, And all the things you may desire cannot compare with her."

Proverbs 31:26 " She opens her mouth with wisdom, And on her tongue *is* the law of kindness.."

Proverbs. 14:1 "The wise woman builds her house, But the foolish pulls it down with her hands.

Proverbs. 19:13 "A foolish son is the ruin of his father, And the contentions of a wife are a continual dripping."

Proverbs. 21:9 "Better to dwell in a corner of a housetop, Than in a house shared with a contentious woman."

Proverbs. 31: 17-18 "She girds herself with strength, And strengthens her arms. She perceives that her merchandise is good, And her lamp does not go out by night."

Proverbs.21:19 "Better to dwell in the wilderness, Than with a contentious and angry woman."

Proverbs. 31: 16 "She considers a field and buys it; From her profits she plants a vineyard."

Proverbs.12:4 "An excellent wife is the crown of her husband, But she who causes shame is like rottenness in his bones."

Proverbs. 31:19 "She stretches out her hands to the distaff, And her hand holds the spindle.

Proverbs. 31:10-12 "Who can find a virtuous wife? For her worth is far above rubies. The heart of her husband safely trusts her; So he will have no lack of gain. She does him good and not evil All the days of her life."

Proverbs. 31:13-15 "She seeks wool and flax, And willingly works with her hands. She is like the merchant ships, She brings her food from afar. She also rises while it is yet night, And provides food for her household, And a portion for her maidservants."

Proverbs.31:26 "She opens her mouth with wisdom, And on her tongue is the law of kindness."

Ephesians.5:22-23 "Wives, submit to your own husbands, as to the Lord. For the husband is head of the wife, as also Christ is head of the church; and He is the Savior of the body."

1st Peter. 3:1-2 "Wives, likewise, be submissive to your own husbands, that even if some do not obey the word, they, without a word, may be won by the conduct of their wives, when they observe your chaste conduct accompanied by fear."

Titus. 2:3-5 "The older women likewise, that they be reverent in behaviour, not slanderers, not given to much wine, teachers of good things— that they admonish the young women to love their husbands, to love their children to be discreet, chaste, homemakers, good, obedient to their own husbands, that the word of God may not be blasphemed."

1ˢᵗ Tim. 2:9-10 "In like manner also, that the women adorn themselves in modest apparel, with propriety and moderation, not with braided hair or gold or pearls or costly clothing, but, which is proper for women professing godliness, with good works."

1ˢᵗ Cor. 11:3 "But I want you to know that the head of every man is Christ, the head of woman is man, and the head of Christ is God."

1ˢᵗ Tim.5:14 "Therefore I desire that the younger widows marry, bear children, manage the house, give no opportunity to the adversary to speak reproachfully."

Col.3:18-19 "Wives, submit to your own husbands, as is fitting in the Lord. Husbands, love your wives and do not be bitter toward them."

Proverbs.31:27 "She watches over the ways of her household, And does not eat the bread of idleness."

2ⁿᵈ Tim.1:5 "when I call to remembrance the genuine faith that is in you, which dwelt first in your grandmother Lois and your mother Eunice, and I am persuaded is in you also."

Proverbs.31:28 "Her children rise up and call her blessed; Her husband also, and he praises her."

Proverbs.31:25 "Strength and honour are her clothing; She shall rejoice in time to come."

Proverbs 18:22 "He who finds a wife finds a good thing, And obtains favour from the LORD."

Proverbs.23:22 "Listen to your father who begot you, And do not despise your mother when she is old."

Proverbs.4:6 "Do not forsake her, and she will preserve you; Love her, and she will keep you."

Proverbs.11:22 "As a ring of gold in a swine's snout, So is a lovely woman who lacks discretion."

Proverbs.31:21 "She is not afraid of snow for her household, For all her household is clothed with scarlet."

BIBLIOGRAPHY

The Bible

Jakes, T.D.2002.*God's Leading Lady: Out of the Shadows and into the Light.* Berkley.

Sandberg, Sheryl & Scovell, Nell. 2013.Lean *In: Women, Work, and the Will to Lead.* Alfred A. Knopf.

Stigel, V. Herta. 2011.The *Mountain Within: Leadership Lessons and Inspiration for Your Climb to the Top.* McGraw-Hill Eductaion.

Scott, Janny. 2011.A *Singular Woman: The Untold Story of Barack Obama's Mother.* Riverhead Books.

Meyer, Joyce. 2010.Eat *the Cookie... Buy the Shoes: Giving Yourself Permission to Lighten Up.* FaithWords.

Karssen, Gien. 1974.Her *Name is Woman.* NavPress Publishing Group.

Live By Faith by Rev. Teresa Wairimu

Yancey, Philip. 2002. Where *Is God When It Hurts?* Zondervan.

Shellenberger, Susie & Gowler, Kathy. 2007. What *Your Daughter Isn't Telling You: Expert Insight Into the World of Teen Girls*. Bethany House Publishers.

Boundaries by Pastor Sammy Hinn

Covey, R. Stephen. 2004. The *7 Habits of Highly Effective People: Powerful Lessons in Personal Change*. Free Press.

Dr. D. W. Ekstrand, 2012. The Influence Parents have on their Children. Accessed on 28th July, 2020 http://www.thetransformedsoul.com/additional-studies

Sasha, 2016: The influence of a good teacher can never be erased. Accessed on 28th July, 2020 https://mirrorgirlblog.wordpress.com/2016/09/17/

Leslie Becker-Phelps, PHD, 2005; Ways your Friends Influence your Future. Accessed on https://blogs.webmd.com/relationships/20160928

Brandon Thomas, 2008: Does past experience affect what we see or what we do? accessed on 29th July, 2020 https://www.researchgate.net/post/Does_past_experience

Art Markman, Ph.D. 2011: Your View of the Future Is Shaped by the Past. Accessed on 29th July, 2020 https://www.psychologytoday.com/us/blog/ulterior-motives/201108

Orit E. Tykocinski and Andreas Ortmann. 2011: The Lingering Effects of Our Past Experiences: The Sunk-Cost Fallacy and the Inaction-Inertia Effect. Accessed on 29th July, 2020 http://portal.idc.ac.il/he/schools/psychology/

Claire Newton. 2020: Destiny: Action or Accident? Accessed on 29th July 2020 http://www.clairenewton.co.za/my-articles/destiny-action-or-accident.html

Sandra Dawes.2014. Following your inner voice. Accessed on 29th July, 2020 https://embraceurdestiny.com/2014/01/29/following-your-inner-voice/

Kenneth Copeland, 2018. Ways to Know If You're Hearing God's Voice. Accessed on 29th July,2020 https://blog.kcm.org/4-ways-know-youre-hearing-gods-voice/

Pincott Jena E, 2019. Silencing Your Inner Critic, accessed on 29th July, 2020 https://www.psychologytoday.com/us/articles/201903/silencing-your-inner-critic

Bonnie Badenoch, Ph.D. 2010. Critical Inner Voice. Accessed on 29th July, 2020 https://www.psychalive.org/critical-inner-voice/